Honda CRF
Performance
Handbook

Honda CRF
Performance Handbook

Eric Gorr

MOTORBOOKS

First published in 2006 by Motorbooks, an imprint of
MBI Publishing Company, Galtier Plaza, Suite 200,
380 Jackson Street, St. Paul, MN 55101-3885 USA

MBI Publishing Company titles are also available at
discounts in bulk quantity for industrial or sales-
promotional use. For details write to Special Sales
Manager at MBI Publishing Company, Galtier Plaza,
Suite 200, 380 Jackson Street, St. Paul, MN
55101-3885 USA

Library of Congress Cataloging-in-Publication Data

Gorr, Eric, 1957-
  Honda CRF performance project handbook / by Eric
Gorr.
     p. cm.
  Includes bibliographical references and index.
  ISBN-13: 978-0-7603-2409-7 (pbk. : alk. paper)
  ISBN-10: 0-7603-2409-3 (pbk. : alk. paper)
  1. Honda motorcycle--Performance. 2. Trail bikes--
Performance. I.
Title.
  TL448.H6.G67 2006
  629.227'5--dc22

                                   2006010886

Editor: Lee Klancher
Designer: LeAnn Kuhlmann

Printed in China

On the cover: Mike LaRocco on his Honda CRF450R.
The veteran rider is one of the legends of the sport,
and has been racing motocross professionally for
20 years. *Simon Cudby*

On the back cover: Fluidyne radiators are available
with colored CV4 silicon hoses.

On the frontispiece: Jeremy circa 2006. He raced select
events, with his best finish a respectable fourth-place
effort at San Diego in February. *Ken Faught*

On the title pages: The sound of Supercross has been
transformed from the shriek of two-stroke motors to
the booming exhaust notes of four-stroke engines.
Ken Faught

About the Author

Eric Gorr is an author, inventor, and engineer from
Chicago. Eric started work as a motorcycle mechanic
and amateur racer and quickly advanced to performance machining. By age 23 Eric was awarded two U.S.
patents on technology related to internal combustion
engines. As a dirt bike design innovator, Eric built a
long travel 1974 YZ250A in high school shop class,
and in 1981 he designed an early version of a modern
low CG and narrow motocross bike. Eric's business,
Forward Motion, serves as a field data collection center for all of his writings that started in a 1981 issue of
Dirt Bike magazine. By 1993 Eric became a popular
techno-journalist with over a million readers worldwide with technical features in *Dirt Rider* (USA), *Dirt
Bike Rider* and *Performance Bike* (UK), *MX Sport*
(Spain), and *Australasian Dirt Bike* magazine in Aus-
tralia. In 1996 Eric worked with Motorbooks to write
the best-selling, award-winning book *MX & Off-Road
Performance Handbook*, which is in its third edition.
Watch for future Motorbooks by Eric on performance
projects and minicycles. Internet support for this book
is available on Eric's website, www.forwardmotion.com.

Contents

Acknowledgments

There are so many to thank for help in producing this book. The biggest influence is the loyal army of CRF owners who called me with things ranging from chronic mechanical problems, shade-tree fixes, questions about how aftermarket products worked, and all the important field data that helps me sort out all the things that CRF owners want to read in a project book.

Lee Klancher, the acquisitions editor at MBI Publishing who is responsible for their off-road motorcycle product line, was the original advocate of my first performance handbook and this new line of model-specific, off-road performance project books. Lee is the driving force behind this book, and he helped keep me on track. Our creative collaboration always produces cutting-edge tech.

Eric Bleed of DeCal Racing helped with the chapter on graphic customization.

Steve Janisch helped to accumulate field data from his son Jesse's racing program. Jesse is a professional roadracer with a background in motocross, supermoto, and dirt track.

Steve Johnson from Wiseco has been a big supporter of my work, providing insight into their extensive research on piston and clutch designs. Steve has the enviable job of working with top racers and teams and coordinating product changes to continually improve performance.

Karel Kramer, the senior editor of *Dirt Rider* magazine for the past three decades, has given me the opportunity to write feature tech articles for a global audience.

Curt Leaverton, the owner of Hot Cams, Pivot Works, and Hot Rods, provided product samples and his engineering expertise on everything from bearings to cams to crankshafts.

Mike Perry of Kibblewhite Performance Machine provided sample parts and the benefit of his vast experience of valvetrains and cylinder head performance machining.

Scott Reath of U.S. Chrome provided help with cylinder plating on my experimental big-bore kits.

Rich Rohrich has been my sounding board for crackpot ideas for years. His experience as the supermoderator at DirtRider.Net helps ground my writing and makes it more reader-friendly.

Tyler Smulders, a pro motocross racer from Watertown, Wisconsin, has been my CRF test rider since the CRF450 first hit the market. Together we've tested every product made for the CRFs. Tyler helped me determine the typical service intervals of all the components on a CRF. At my workshop, the term "Tylerized" means that a product has been beat into submission or smoked entirely.

A. J. Waggoner and Greg Foster of Service Honda, custom dirt-bike builders of the AF500 and Junior, advised me on specific Honda model changes, improved and superseded Honda part numbers, and their experiences supporting the Subway Honda motocross team.

Jeremy Wilkey of MX-Tech, my longtime collaborator, helped out on the suspension chapter of this book as well as my current *Motocross and Off-Road Performance Handbook.*

Introduction

With the advent of four-stroke dirt bikes, we've seen a boost in technology, an influx of new riders into the sport, and explosive growth in new product development by aftermarket manufacturers. Riders have embraced these bikes wholeheartedly for their tractable power. The new four-strokes are the most competitive bikes on the track, and they have changed the sound and feel of motocross racing.

The bikes have also changed the way that riders view four-strokes. The four-stroke off-road bikes of old—Honda XRs, Suzuki DRZs, and the like—are legendary for slow-revving power, heavy weight, and rock-solid reliability even in the face of abysmal maintenance. The new four-strokes rev quickly, make quick-revving, explosive power, and, well, they require significant maintenance. You could ride an XR400 forever by only changing the oil periodically. A new four-stroke, on the other hand, is a much more high-performance animal that requires the same attention lavished on two-stroke race bikes. Oil needs to be changed religiously, and the valves and top ends will require regular rebuilds.

The part that has shocked some four-stroke fans is the cost of the rebuilds. Two-stroke top end rebuilds are something that the home mechanic can do in an afternoon for about $100–$150. Even at a shop, rebuilding a two-stroke top end is not terribly expensive.

Four-stroke top ends are more complex to rebuild, and they can cost $1,500–2,500 to have done at a shop. This has opened some eyes to the fact that this new level of performance comes at a price, and the new performance four-strokes have more in common with the two-strokes of old than the stone-reliable XR400s and DRZ400s running around the country.

This is not to say that you shouldn't buy a Honda CRF. They are some of the best tools available for the job. If you want to win, or simply want to ride the best, they are ideal choices.

What this book does is show you both how to get the best performance out of your CRF, and how to maintain it properly to keep it running. Consider this a bridge between your factory service manual and a super-deluxe product installation guide. Unlike the factory manual, we will include maintenance and performance upgrades. We'll tell you when to use aftermarket parts to increase the longevity of your bike, and when to use factory parts.

This book will also tell you the advantages and disadvantages of aftermarket goodies. Too many magazines profile performance parts without telling you the difficulty of installation, and the drawbacks of the upgrades. But magazine editors are beholden to advertisers. Book authors are not. So this book will give you frank recommendations of how to make your Honda CRF perform its best, and how to make it last without costing you all-too-frequent and overly expensive rebuilds.

Bear in mind that this performance project book is not intended to replace the factory service manual for your model bike. Each chapter starts with basic maintenance, because a great time to install hop-up parts is during your routine maintenance. The factory service manual is ideal for quick references on part wear tolerances and torque specifications. This is a book for anyone who wants to take control of custom projects.

The first book in this series, *YZF Performance Projects*, which Ken Faught and I wrote, was introduced in late 2005 and is quickly becoming the hop-up bible for Yamaha owners. We've made changes to the format of the CRF book based on our experiences with the YZF book. The major difference in this CRF book is that we have a lot more technical detail in the CRF book. The book is intended for owners who want to know more about their bike, or for those hands-on owners willing to do most of their own wrenching. We also grouped the performance projects by component. The emphasis is on starting out with basic maintenance first, then combining it with a performance-accessory installation guide.

The CRF450 was introduced in 2002, so we've accumulated quite a bit of field data on all the CRFs over the years, including information on what breaks when, how to fix it right the first time, and which aftermarket products work the best.

Best of luck with all your CRF performance projects. You've got one of the best bikes in the world, and this book will help you tailor it to your riding needs, not to mention keep it out of the shop and out on the track!

—Eric Gorr

SECTION 1
GETTING STARTED

Chapter 1
CRF BUYER'S GUIDE

There are as many choices for buying a CRF as there are personalities of riders. Before you consider making a deal on a bike, think about what type of person you are. If you have the finances and a perfect bike is important to you, buy a new bike from a Honda dealer. If you are a thrifty, do-it-yourself handyman, then a used or nonrunning bike will afford you the chance to customize it to your needs for a relatively good price. The fix-it-up scenario can be a good deal, but it's a gamble. This book will help you determine the critical points to check on a used CRF. Motorcycles can be purchased used or new from dealers, the news-paper, and online sites like eBay. The alternative places to buy include bank repossessions and race teams. If you are a fan of a certain rider, you can write a letter to the team manager and inquire about the price of buying a used race bike. Oftentimes these race bikes will be kitted out with graphics, suspension and engine mods, or other sponsored accessories.

R or X?
One of the decisions you need to make is whether to buy an R race bike or an X off-road model. The R models are better suited for motocross tracks. They

A Honda dealer is the best place to see the full line of CRF models.

A CRF450X features electric start, lights, and a detuned R engine.

are lighter, have more explosive power, and are more stiffly sprung. They have narrow-ratio transmissions, no lights, kick starts, and smaller gas tanks. If you are spending most of your time on motocross tracks or even just out play riding, the R model is probably a better fit. Some off-road racers prefer to convert R models rather than using X models, but bear in mind that this is an expensive process.

The X models are designed for off-road use (meaning enduro or hare scramble competition, or trail riding). They have electric start, which is a huge plus with a four-stroke, as four-stroke engines are harder to start than two-strokes. On the trail, the electric starter is a huge advantage if you stall the bike in a place where it is awkward to start, like on a hill or while crossing a log. Also, the X models come with a headlight and taillight as standard equipment. The gear ratios are wider, meaning you have a low first gear suitable for crawling up and over off-road obstacles, and the top gear allows you more speed for open

The CRF450R is a competitive motocross bike with potential for other motorcycle sports.

Franchised dealers often take used bikes on trade. Because floor space is at a premium, you might get a better deal than with a private party.

sections of trail. The engine power on the X models will be a bit milder, with more power in the low part of the rev range.

The X models are better suited to riding trails, and easier to ride for long periods of time. You'll give up a bit of horsepower and weight, but the payoff is worth it for most off-road riders. If you are intending to make the bike street legal, the X models are a much better choice. Note that shorter riders or those with bad knees may want to consider the X models even for motocross use just for the electric start.

250 Lightweight or 450 Heavyweight

The displacement of a CRF is an important consideration, and there are many factors you'll need to take into account, ranging from skill level, body weight and size, demands of the terrain, and personal preferences. If you're just starting in dirt biking or are returning to the sport after a long layoff period, then a 250 is a great choice. The light weight and forgiving power-band will help you improve your riding skills with confidence. The 450 is a good choice for riders with experience and guys with a bigger stature, even if they are beginners.

Another consideration in choosing the displacement of a CRF is longevity. The 450 is built more as a heavy-duty machine than the 250. If you plan to ride more than 50 hours per year, the 450 will hold up better and cost less per hour to operate.

Check the air filter and spark plug of used bikes for signs of abuse and neglect.

Race Bikes and Rats

Bikes that are trail ridden usually have more time on them than race bikes. Used race bikes purchased from expert riders are normally well maintained and have relatively little running time. Expert riders usually have several sponsors, so their bikes may have extra accessories, such as suspension or engine modifications, stiffer springs, good tires and brakes, or a special pipe. Don't be afraid of race bikes; they can be a good bargain.

"Rats" are bikes that have been crashed and abused. Normally, they will have loads of serious mechanical problems, but you can buy rat bikes very cheaply. If you are mechanically confident, you can do well to repair and resell these bikes. Sometimes franchised motorcycle dealers will have dirt bikes that were abandoned by their owners because the repair estimate was too expensive. In most cases the dealer just wants to get rid of the bikes, because they take up space in the service department. Rat bikes can be a bargain for the skilled mechanic who gets a good discount on parts and accessories. However, many people who buy one of these bikes, thinking it's a cheap way to get into dirt bikes, later find out that the cost to repair the bike is more than a year-old race bike.

Evaluating and Testing Used Bikes

The excitement of the first test ride can hide potential mechanical problems that can cost big money once you're down the road. Buying a used dirt bike can be very risky, because the most expensive components to repair are the ones that are most difficult to see. There are some tricks to examining a used dirt bike and estimating the cost of repairs, so you can gain bargaining leverage with the seller. What follows are the most important clues.

Oil Leaks

Examine the fork tubes and shock shafts. Seal leaks in the front may be due to rock dents. Run your fingers across the fork tubes and feel for sharp scratches. Replacing fork seals and wipers is an annual service; bad fork tubes can run as high as $700 a set. If you see oil leaking from the shock shaft, that is very serious, and repairs start at about $175.

There are several places where engine oil leaks can occur. Check the bottom of the crankcases. If a bike is power-washed clean, sprinkle some white baby powder on the cases to spot-check for oil leaks. Leaks are likely to originate from the drain bolts, side covers, and countershaft. Cases get hit with rocks, drain bolts are often overtightened, and countershaft seals get shredded from debris carried by the chain. Cracks in

the cases can be very expensive. Although Honda sells case halves relatively cheaply, you must present a valid manufacturer's statement of origin (MSO) with the old crankcase halves in order for a Honda dealer to sell you a replacement part.

A simple way to check the piston's condition is by looking for oil buildup in the intake air boot. Remove

Bring a small compressor and a Motion Pro leak-down pressure tester to check the condition of the engine's top end. Leakage over 20 percent could cost you upwards of $1,000.

A mechanical stethoscope can help you listen inside the engine for potential screeching bearings or worn-out valvetrain parts. You can buy a mechanical stethoscope at any auto parts store.

seal and the water pump seal. When the coolant side seal fails, the coolant pours out the bottom of the cover. Check the bottom of the cover for weeping with the engine running. Water pumps must be rebuilt completely with a new shaft, bearing, gaskets, and seals. It is a common problem for the 450 and costs about $90 in parts. The radiators on CRFs are very expensive but cheaply built. They are prone to bending when the bike crashes on its sides. The fittings and the tanks may develop tiny leaks, so remove the radiator shrouds and check each radiator. Aftermarket radiators like Fluidyne are better built, less expensive than Honda parts, and offer an improvement in cooling performance for $375 a set.

Examine the Air Filter

Check the air filter for holes or tears where dirt may have entered the engine. Examine the fire screen for black spots. This could be an indication that the intake valves are worn and not sealing. Look for thick deposits of dark oil in the air boot. Check the vent hose to make sure it is attached to the fitting in the air boot. If the connection is open, dirt can bypass the air

the air filter and run your finger down from the top of the inside of the air boot to check for excessive dark oil. If the piston rings are worn, combustion pressure will blow by the rings and into the crankcase. The vent tube on the top of the valve cover is attached to the top of the air boot, and it allows blow-by gases to recirculate into the incoming mixture stream. If the bike smokes badly from the tailpipe, the piston and rings are definitely worn. A top end rebuild can run as high as $500.

Coolant Leaks

Most late-model dirt bikes have a failsafe system that protects the transmission from the coolant. There is a weep hole in the bottom of the water pump cover. The hole is drilled into a free space between the transmission

These 2004 CRF250R/X have problems with the skirts cracking. Honda changed the shape of the skirt on 2005 and later models. These samples have been sprayed with Magnaflux dye to locate cracks in the aluminum cylinder block.

Thumper Racing makes a big-bore kit to fix the skirt-cracking problem of the 2004 CRF250R/X. Thumper installs a longer steel wet-liner for greater stability and increased displacement.

filter and cause engine damage. Repairing the top end on a four-stroke ranges from $200 to $700, and that's if *you* do most of the labor.

Listen for Bad Noises

Squeaks, howls, and grinding sounds are bad noises, which can cost you a lot of money. Bad noises can be heard with the engine off, at idle, when revved, and when riding in gear. With the engine off, bounce up and down on the bike and listen for squeaks in the shock linkage and swingarm bearings. The hideous, rusty screech of worn-out bearings can ring to the tune of $150 in a complete Pivot Works rebuild kit. If the rear end tops out hard and makes a clunk, it could be a sign that the shock bladder is blown. A shock rebuild will start at about $175.

Roll the bike forward and backward. Listen for squeaks from the brake discs; if they are intermittent, the discs could be bent. Check the discs for deep scratches that could indicate the bike was ridden with pads worn to the backing plate. If the wheel bearings are worn, the wheels may hop or be difficult to roll. New brake pads cost between $20 and $50, discs range from $45 to $150, and wheel bearings are about $30 a set.

Check the chain and sprockets for wear; a bad chain makes a crunching sound and hops on the sprocket teeth. A set of chain and sprockets runs from $80 to $150.

Grab the front brake lever and rock the bike forward and backward. If you hear and feel a clunking noise through the handlebars, the steering head bearings may need adjustment or repair. Sometimes you can repack the bearings with grease and torque the spanner nut to cure the problem. If the bearings and races need replacement, that could run as much as $150 in parts, plus it's a difficult mechanical task that requires a 20-ton hydraulic press.

Start the engine and wait for it to come down to a stable idle. Use a mechanical stethoscope and touch it to the top and bottom ends and right-side cover of the engine. The stethoscope will magnify and isolate certain noises, like too much clearance in the valvetrain, worn crankshaft bearings, or a bad clutch basket.

Rev the engine slowly and listen for erratic popping and backfiring. If the engine won't take the throttle and it bogs, it could be a sign of a partially clogged carb. Backfiring noises can be a sign of worn or too-tight valve clearance. Problems like these may be repaired cheaply with only the investment of your labor in a valve adjustment and a carb flushing.

Test Riding
Ride the bike and listen for growling noises when you

Wiseco makes aftermarket CRF500 cylinders as well as standard piston kits with higher compression and gas ports. A Pro-Lite high-compression piston gives the most power increase for the money.

let out the clutch. If the bike jumps forward when you put it in first gear with the clutch lever in, then the clutch basket and pressure plate are worn. Honda uses soft cast-aluminum material for the clutch basket and pressure plate. The average life is two seasons. Average replacement cost of higher-quality aftermarket parts runs from $200 to $500.

To test the engine performance, make sure it shifts through all the gears, then put it in third gear and roll on the throttle from the bottom. It should run progressively, not jerky. Bogging and popping can be caused by things like dirty carb jets or valves that have too little clearance. These problems may be repaired with a few hours of labor. Bogging and popping are common problems that vary in repair costs.

Test the brakes to make sure the bike tracks straight to a stop. If the frame is bent or the steering and swingarm bearings are worn, the bike will track side-to-side abruptly.

Negotiating a Fair Price for a Dirt Bike
Whenever you check out a used bike, try to curb your enthusiasm. That will enable you to look at the bike objectively, and see all the hidden things that could cost a lot to repair. You can clip ads from dirt bike magazines that feature discount prices for OEM parts. An excellent tool for negotiating the price of a used bike is a Blue Book guide. These guides are available from libraries or on the Internet. Although the prices listed for used dirt bikes do not reflect regional market values, they are a good indicator for determining if the seller is way out of line on the price of a bike. Normally, the Blue Book value will be lower than the typical price you would pay for a used bike; motorcycle shops use these guides to negotiate trade-in value. Before you try to barter on the price of a bike with an individual, ask to see the MSO: it's like a title for a dirt bike. If he or she doesn't have it, the bike may be stolen, or perhaps state sales tax was never paid on the vehicle. If you buy the bike and try to register it, you may have to pay the original sales tax for your state and county. Check the frame and engine for serial number badge plates. If they're missing, pass on the bike.

Here is a list of some of the common CRF flaws and some insight into the types of aftermarket products that offer performance or longevity benefits. Ask the seller for records like invoices on parts installed and service repairs performed on the bike. A new trend is to keep a logbook segmented by engine hours that tracks service intervals and costs. Sellers with logbooks get top dollar for their CRFs.

Flaws and Fixes with Best-Value Mods

This is a list of the known weak points of each CRF model, along with the recommended fixes for those flaws and the modifications that will give the most performance improvement for your money.

2002 CRF450R

Flaws: Soft valvetrain parts, worn cam chain tensioner, leaky water pump, weak low-end power, slow steering, spongy clutch

Fixes: Steel valvetrain, 2004 cam chain tensioner, replace water pump parts as a set, Stage 1 cam, aftermarket triple clamps with more offset

Best-Value Mods: Hot Cam 1, Wiseco high-compression piston, RG3 triple clamps, Fastway clutch cable holder, oversize foot pegs

2003–2004 CRF450R

Flaws: Soft clutch baskets get notched quickly, engine runs hot, radiators crush easily, cam chain tensioner (on 2003 model)

Fixes: Forged or billet clutch baskets and pressure plates, high-flow water pump kit, oversized radiators, 2004 tensioner

Best-Value Mods: Wiseco or Hinson clutches, Boyesen impellor and cover, Fluidyne radiators

2004 CRF250R/X

Flaws: Weak low-end power, frequent valvetrain wear, cylinder cracks, valve seats chip

Fixes: 2006 CRF cylinder head, steel valves, 2005 cylinder

Best-Value Mods: 2006 CRF cylinder and head, Black Diamond stainless steel valves, Hinson Pro clutch kit, knurled carb adjuster, Thumper Racing 270 kit, Hot Cam

2005–2006 CRF250R/X

Flaws: Leaky seal between crank and transmission, weak clutch

Fixes: New Honda seal, complete clutch

Best-Value Mods: Hinson Pro clutch kit, Hot Cam, Black Diamond valves

2005–2006 CRF450R

Flaws: Leaky seal between crank and transmission, intake valves wear

Fixes: New Honda seal

Best-Value Mods: Boyesen Quick-Shot, RG3 top clamp, Hot Cam 1

Honda 2004–2006 CRF250R/X

The 250 is a high-revving, high-maintenance dirt bike. The big problem with the Honda CRF250 is the valve-train. The springs aren't adequate and the valves bounce against the seat, mushrooming the valve and seat. Other problems include chipped valve seats and worn exhaust guides. Rather than try to repair the cylinder head, it's best to buy a new 2006 R head, because it interchanges with the 2004 and 2005 R and X models. The stock 2006 CRF250R head has constricted ports that help low and midrange throttle response. The valve seat material is softer, which may help the stock valves last longer. Regarding valvetrain choices, there are two schools of thought: stainless steel for longevity, and titanium for performance. KPM and Ferrea specialize in stainless valves, and Xceldyne and Del West specialize in titanium. Prices range from $31 for stainless valves and $80 for stock titanium to $130 for aftermarket titanium.

The 2004 cylinder is too thin at the skirt, and it will eventually crack. The 2005 cylinder is the best replacement choice. By grinding a groove in the cylinder for clearance of the 2004 oil spray bar, it is possible to bolt the 2005 cylinder on the 2004 engine. If you're looking for a sturdy, big-bore kit with a long service interval on piston changes, an aftermarket alternative is Thumper Racing's 270-cc kit, which features a better piston and an LA Sleeve wet liner. The skirt on the piston and liner have more support area than a stock 2005 cylinder.

The chassis and suspension are the great strengths of the CRF250 models. Narrow, with a low center of gravity, the CRF250 is easy to ride, making it a popular bike for all forms of off-road motorcycling.

Honda 2002–2006 CRF450R/X

Overall, the 450 engine has been a reliable workhorse, with cleverly designed features that reduce the chances of expensive "energetic disassembly" (i.e., blowing up). The weak points are the intake valves and the cam chain tensioner. The symptoms of a worn tensioner are a clacking noise at idle, and worn valves make the bike hard to get started with the kickstarter. The intake valves tend to get cupped from bouncing off the valve seat, and the exhaust valves are prone to corrosion from pump gas. The quality of the stock Honda head is good. The valve guides and seats are very hard and wear-resistant. The rocker arm and cam bearing are replaceable and can be checked by simply turning the bearing or roller and feeling for notchy movement. The ball bearings that support the camshaft wear out after a few years and make a lot of valvetrain noises. One of the camshaft bearings is made with the cam, so when it wears you have to replace the camshaft, and order the right-side bearing separately. Hot Cams makes replacement cams in two different performance stages; the Stage 1 cam makes more low to midrange and the Stage 2 cam makes more midrange to top end.

The piston and cylinder are very reliable on the 450s. Piston life averages 75 hours, the cylinder plating 150. If you're a big guy looking for more low end there are two choices: bore and plate the stock cylinder to 478 cc with a Wiseco kit, or buy a complete 500-cc top end kit from Athena.

The overall chassis evolution has changed rapidly from model to model. The 2004 model could be improved with an aftermarket triple clamp, allowing more offset and quicker steering. These changes were incorporated into the 2003 and 2004 models, along with fork and shock valving changes. The 2005 model marked Honda's move toward a lighter and narrower chassis with a lower center of gravity. The 2005 and newer 450 uses the 250 chassis, creating a high demand for these bikes on the used market.

Once you've made the choice of which year and model CRF best suits your needs and budget, you should follow the chapters in this book to evaluate each major engine and chassis component. From there you can decide which performance projects will satisfy the bike's maintenance needs and your performance needs.

Cam chain tensioners are a weak point of the 2002–2003 CRF450R. You can test a tensioner by pressing it into your hand while wiggling it. If the plunger collapses, it's junk. Replace it with the redesigned 2004 tensioner for about $45.

Chapter 2
TOOL SETS AND WORKSHOP

Making the commitment to trying the performance projects in this book requires an investment in tools. Having the right tools can make a tough job less frustrating and save you money in labor and costly mistakes.

Where to Buy Tools

Here are lists of tools for different types of maintenance applications. You can spend a fortune on good tools or buy a bunch of cheap tools that wear out fast—the choice is yours. But you have the rip-off factor to consider. If you have expensive tools, people will borrow them and conveniently forget to return them.

I believe in buying inexpensive tools for the weather-exposure and regular-maintenance jobs and expensive, high-quality tools for special jobs and performance tuning in the shop. For routine maintenance

tools such as wrenches and screwdrivers, look to Craftsman (Sears). They make good-quality tools for a low price and you can get free replacements if the tools break.

Harbor Freight sells all sorts of tools like T-handle sets for less than $10. They sell the kind of tools that are supercheap and good for rough use where they are prone to getting lost or stolen.

If you have a secure toolbox and want a better grade of motorcycle tools, five companies sell above-average and premium-grade tools.

Tool Companies

Precision Manufacturing, Kowa Tools, and Motion Pro specialize strictly in motorcycle tools. Precision Manufacturing offers the widest range of tools to start a motorcycle repair business. Kowa Tools is a Japanese

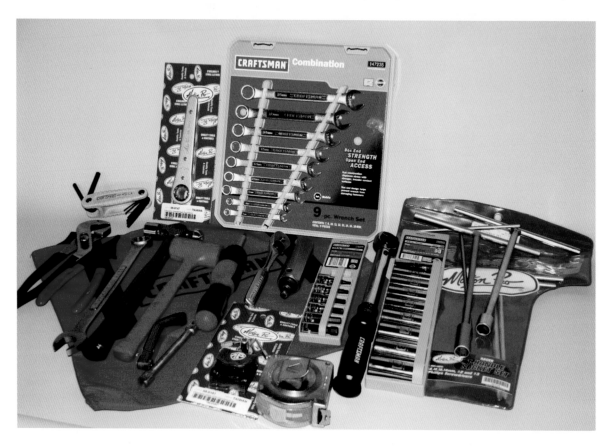

For less than $500 you can buy the right kinds of tools to make the projects in this book easy.

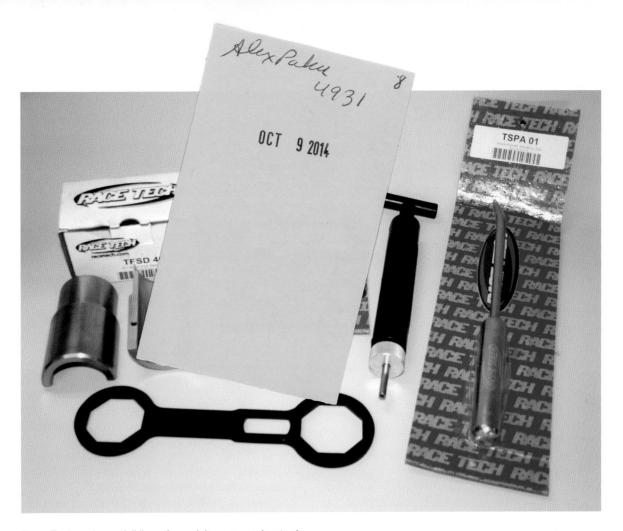

Race Tech makes a full line of specialty suspension tools.

company that manufactures special tools for the Big 4 motorcycle companies. Kowa Tools also sells direct to consumers with a mail-order branch in California. Motion Pro has many dirt-bike specialty tools, including four-stroke leak-down testers, nitrogen charging systems, and valve-spring compressors, as well as the biggest selection of pullers and drivers for engine and suspension rebuilding.

Hop-up shops like Race Tech and Pro Circuit offer all the basic T-handle and wrench sets, but Race Tech specializes in the most complete selection of special suspension and chassis tools.

How the Project Legend Works

At the beginning of each project there is a legend that lists the time, tools, and talent you'll need to complete the job, as well as the cost ("tab"), parts you'll need, and benefits you'll reap from that particular job. Pay close attention to the "talent" category. Listed from one to five stars, each corresponds approximately to the level of skill recommended—and a tool set. A one-star talent rating means you'll be able to complete the job with minimal skill, the tools from Set 1 below, and any special tools or parts you may need for the job. On the other hand, a four-star talent rating means you'll need considerable skill as well as the tools from Sets 4, 3, 2, and 1, in addition to any special tools or parts the job may require.

Below are lists of tools for you to compare to what's in your toolbox. You may need to go tool shopping before you attempt some of your favorite projects.

Tool Set 1

This set includes the tools needed to perform basic maintenance tasks.

1. Special wrenches: spark plug, spoke, rear axle, and carb main-jet wrenches
2. Combination wrenches in sizes of 8–19 mm
3. T-handles in sizes of 8–17 mm
4. Screwdrivers: one wide and one narrow flat-blade (10 and 3 mm wide) and a #2 and a #3 Phillips
5. Allen wrench combination set (2.5, 4, 5, 6, 8, and 10 mm)
6. Impact driver with a 3/8-inch drive
7. Combination snap-ring pliers
8. Miscellaneous tools: feeler gauge, air-pressure gauge, measuring tape, cable-lubing tool, chain brush, pliers, and plastic mallet

Tool Set 1 includes the most basic tools that you will need to maintain your bike.

Tool Set 2

This set includes more sockets and tools for annual maintenance.

1. 3/8-inch ratchet wrench and sockets in six-point shallow socket sizes of 8, 10, 12, 14, 17, 19, 22, 24, 27, 30, and 32 mm and Allen sockets in sizes of 2.5, 4, 5, 6, 8, and 10 mm
2. Combination wrenches in sizes of 22, 24, 27, and 32 mm
3. Needle-nose and channel-lock pliers, side cutters, chain clamp, and tweezers
4. Hand-powered, electric, and/or pneumatic impact driver

5. Two torque wrenches (inch-pounds and foot-pounds)
6. Ball-peen hammer and plastic mallet
7. Rat-tail, big-flat-fine and triangular files, set of needle files, and a thread file
8. Large- and small-diameter round punches and a 1/4-inch-wide flat chisel
9. Mini parts washer
10. Propane torch
11. Drill
12. Air compressor

Tool Set 2 includes tools to handle most of the projects rated between one and four stars.

For the projects rated three to five stars, you'll need at least a small air compressor and either a pneumatic or electric impact wrench. A heat gun or propane torch come in handy for breaking parts loose too.

Tool Set 3

These are tools for tougher-than-average projects, including major engine rebuilding.
1. Bearing and seal driver set
2. Dial caliper
3. Valve-spring compressor
4. Crankcase-splitting tool
5. Bench vise with aluminum jaws
6. Flywheel puller
7. Dial caliper
8. Moto-Tool grinder

Tool Set 4

This tool set includes suspension-rebuilding tools.
1. Scribe set
2. Oil-level setting tool
3. Nitrogen tank and pressure regulator
4. Bladder-cap remover
5. Special wrenches and sockets
6. Shaft blocks

Tool Set 5

This tool set includes machine tools common to a motorcycle shop.
1. Bench lathe
2. Lathe/mill
3. Hydraulic press

How to Outfit Your Workshop

It's difficult to work on your bike when you don't have the tools. It's even worse when you don't have a place to work on your bike. Reserving a small place in your garage, shed, basement, or even at a rental storage locker is the most basic need. Making the most of that space and providing a measure of security and organization takes a bit of creativity.

Here is an inexpensive solution to the problem of organizing your tools and workshop. Think about the things you need: a solid bench, a vise, a parts washer, and a safe place to store your tools and parts. In previous editions I suggested using a metal motorcycle crate as a foundation for a workbench, but now there is a much better alternative. Pallet racks used to be exclusive to warehouses, but the latest trend in motorcycle dealer service departments is to buy the smaller pallet racks marketed at home improvement stores. These pallet racks are available in kit-piece form so you can customize the height, width, and depth to fit the space you have available. For about $120 you can buy a rack that is 72 inches tall, 96 inches wide, and 24 inches deep. The side Z-beams are notched so you can set the shelf and bench heights to your ergonomic needs. Additionally, there are several other ways to customize a pallet rack, by adding wheels to make it mobile, fitting a power strip in the frame rails, enclosing it for security, fitting a tool box or cabinets, adding a parts washer to the bench top, fastening a mini air-compressor, and even installing a refrigerator.

Slat paneling makes a great backing for the workbench, or the paneling can be fastened directly to your garage walls to hold tools.

Environmentally Conscious Methods for Cleaning Parts

Cleaning is a part of dirt biking. Having the right cleaning kit can make it easy to maintain your bike. Choosing the right chemicals and cleaning methods can be environmentally conscious and safer for your health. Many of the maintenance tasks that you'll need to perform on your bike revolve around a parts washer. You'll use it to do preliminary cleaning like degreasing. You can buy the components of the parts washer, the tank and the chemicals relatively cheaply, but the disposal of the chemicals can be expensive. Companies like Safety Kleen offer parts washers on rental, a variety of different chemicals, and disposal service. Their services are fair at about $80 for solvent and the disposal. That's about what it would cost you to either buy the solvent or dispose of it legally. In my shop I rent a Safety Kleen System One parts washer for $145 per month. This machine features a vacuum distillation pump, which cleans the solvent and separates the oil and spooge to a collection chamber that can be drained and recycled responsibly. Many auto parts stores offer free reclamation of one-gallon containers of oil and antifreeze. Antifreeze is an especially dangerous fluid to leave in open containers, particularly if

you have pets. Dogs are attracted to the smell of antifreeze and often drink it, causing a slow death from the poison. With free reclamation services available from auto parts stores and most municipal garages, there is no excuse to leave open containers of these toxic fluids sitting around.

The cleaning chemicals used in parts washers are either mineral spirits solvents or alkaline detergents. Some areas of the country prohibit mineral spirits solvents because of air pollution or flammability considerations. The alkaline detergents are advertised as biodegradable, but don't be fooled into thinking that you can just pour it down the drain when it's spent. As soon as you clean an oily part with it, it's contaminated and fits into a different waste category. The alkaline detergents tend to be harsher on unprotected skin than mineral spirits solvents. In fact, some solvents have lanolin, a skin moisturizer, mixed in with them. Solvents are also graded in flash points. Generally speaking, the higher the flash point, the better the cleaning action. Most local fire departments have the right to inspect your parts washer and specify what type of chemicals you may use, the allowable flash point temperature, and the type of "fusible link" fitted to the tank's lid. Fusible links are used on all dedicated parts washers. They are built into the hinge of the lid and will melt if the solvent catches fire, closing the lid and smothering the fire.

Gloves should always be used when cleaning parts in solvents or detergents. You don't have to wear big clunky gloves anymore; the latest thing is a nitrile glove. They fit like a second skin. Over the years my skin has become hypersensitive to solvents and detergents, yet the tactile nitrile gloves keep my skin from breaking out in a rash. For mechanical and machining tasks, I use Kevlar-reinforced gloves from Ringer Racing. They supply most of the NASCAR teams with gear that offers heat and abrasion protection.

Developing a strategy for cleaning your bike and disposing of waste while protecting yourself is the foundation for performing any of the projects in this book.

Sears Hardware stores have a full line of Craftsmen pallet racks, benches, and cabinets as well as slat paneling. You can customize your home workshop.

SECTION 2
ENGINE PROJECTS

Chapter 3
CARBURETOR

Projects 1–5

- FCR Carb Service
- Quick Carb Flush
- The Mechanics of Jetting
- Troubleshooting Tips
- How to Install a Powerblade or Powernow
- Installing a Boyesen Quick-Shot

PROJECT 1	FCR Carb Service

Time: 20 minutes

Tools: Allen wrenches, screwdrivers, open end wrenches

Talent: ★★

Tab: $0–$10

Parts: Jets

Benefits: Bike runs cleaner

The Kehin FCR carb is the most complex design ever used on dirt bikes. With a set of both air and fuel jets, it's very important to keep an FCR clean inside and out. This chapter will give you an overview of how to clean, adjust, troubleshoot, and improve FCR carbs.

Cleaning, Adjustments, and Routing

Cleaning the outside of the carb will prevent serious internal damage. For external cleaning, never directly power-wash the carb. The strong detergents and pressure from power washing can corrode the fittings, seals, and main body of the carb. Instead, use an aerosol can of nonchlorinated brake cleaner.

Periodic adjustments include the idle screw, pilot screw, accelerator pump, and float level. On a four-stroke engine, the idle speed needs to be adjusted as the bike gets hot and cold or with changes in outside air temperature. The pilot screw is located on the bottom front center of the carb. The screw is prone to vibrating loose and falling out; aftermarket adjusting screws are longer, easy to adjust, and you can easily see that they're in place. The accelerator pump rarely needs adjustment, but its diaphragm needs to be checked annually for damage. The float level can also be checked annually, but it isn't prone to changes in height from usage. Consult your factory service manual for more information on making these adjustments.

The manufacturer's recommended routing path for the throttle cables, fuel inlet, and air vent hoses is shown in the factory service manual. The throttle cables run through wire hoops welded to the right side of the frame and between the radiator and frame. The bottoms of the vent hoses need to be checked and cleaned before every ride. The hoses exit the bottom of the bike and are prone to getting plugged with mud. The split ends help the hoses self-clean.

Above: The Kehin FCR carb is the most complex design ever used on a dirt bike. With a series of corresponding air and fuel jets, it's important to keep dirt from entering through the fuel and air filters. Stale fuel deposits are the biggest problem after a bike is stored for the winter, and requires the carb to be disassembled this far. Every jet must be cleaned and blow-dried with carb cleaner and compressed air.

These jets are accessible by removing the float bowl. The main jet is the hex-shaped one in the middle. The slow jet is the one above the main jet, and the threaded hole for the low-speed mixture screw is above the slow jet. The jet below the main jet is the starter jet.

<table>
<tr><td>**PROJECT 2**</td><td>Quick Carb Flush</td></tr>
</table>

Time: 20 minutes

Tools: Your brain

Talent: ★

Tab: Free

Parts: none

Benefits: Removes fuel deposits and dirt from carburetor

Carb flushing is a procedure that should be performed whenever the bike has sat for months or when dirt bypasses the air filter. While this is no substitute for a thorough disassembly and cleaning, it's a fast way to flush old gummy fuel deposits and dirt from key areas like the fuel inlet valve and jets.

To perform a quick carb flush, start by removing the seat and subframe. The subframe can be removed by first loosening the clamps on the air intake boot and the exhaust pipe junction. Detach the air vent and fuel hoses from the left side of the carb. Loosen and remove the 17-mm drain bolt located on the bottom of the carb. Carefully remove the low-speed mixture screw. It consists of a needle screw, spring, washer, and O-ring. Lay a small foil pan under the carb to collect the tiny parts during removal of the screw. If the O-ring and washer don't come out with the screw, they may come out during flushing, so leave the tray in place.

Use carb and choke cleaner with the tube nozzle to flush out these passages in this order: vent tube, fuel inlet, and air inlet port in the back of the carb where the air boot attaches. The air inlet port is the most vulnerable area of the carb, because filter oil and dirt run down the air tube and collect in that port.

Above right: A quick carb flush involves squirting non-chlorinated brake cleaner through outside ports in order to flush air and fuel jets down into the open float bowl for drainage. Take care to flush the brake cleaner into a shop towel for disposal.

Right: The accelerator pump used a rubber diaphragm to pump the fuel through the chamber and up the stack. Check the diaphragm for peeling; some fuel additives can damage it.

PROJECT 3 | The Mechanics of Jetting

Time: 20 minutes

Tools: Your brain

Talent: ★

Tab: Free

Parts: None

Benefits: Read this and you'll have a better understanding of carburetion and jetting

The FCR carb is designed so you can make most of the jetting changes right on the bike with only minor mechanical work like removing the seat and fuel tank.

There are three main fuel/air circuits of the carb that correspond to throttle ranges of closed to 1/3, 1/3 to 2/3, and 2/3 to wide open. Marking the throttle housing and grip with a piece of brightly colored tape helps you to determine what throttle position you're in so you can tell if the jetting is rich or lean.

The pilot circuit of the carb controls the fuel/air flow in the first 1/3 of the throttle range. The initial throttle response is the most critical, because that is where the throttle must be applied to handle obstacles like whoops, corners, and landing from jumps. The pilot circuit uses a fuel jet, air jet, and mixture screw. The mixture screw allows the most control over the circuit, and can be adjusted with a straight-blade screwdriver. Turning the screw clockwise (looking up from underneath the carb) will lean the mixture, and turning it counterclockwise will richen the mixture. The range of the pilot screw is about two and a half turns, and the standard setting is one turn out from closed. Turning the pilot screw all the way in or out to effect a change in performance is an indication that you need to change the pilot fuel jet. If changes in the pilot fuel jet help, but you run out of range (jet number size), that is an indication that you need to change the pilot air jet, located in the air bell of the carb.

The jet needle, located in the throttle valve of the carb, mainly controls the middle third of the throttle range. The jet needle has seven clip notches but only the middle three are really effective. Removing the top cover of the carb and unthreading the 4-mm Allen bolt allows access to the jet needle. The needle can be lifted up out the top of the throttle valve. Raising the clip position will lower the needle and lean the mixture. Lowering the clip position will enable more fuel

The mixture screw regulates the air and fuel slow jets. The original screw fits up into the cavity, and the aftermarket screws are longer with large knurled knobs for quick adjustment. Oftentimes, the original mixture screws will fall out and cause the engine to misfire at slow speeds. If you buy an aftermarket mixture screw, make sure that the original spring, washer, and O-ring that seat in the cavity are in good shape.

Chapter 4
TOP END REBUILDING PROJECTS

Projects 6–9

- How to Rebuild a Top End
- Installing an Aftermarket High-Compression Piston Kit
- How to Install a Black Diamond Valvetrain Kit
- Installing a Hot Cam on a CRF450

The top end of a four-stroke CRF engine includes the cylinder, piston, head, cam, and valvetrain parts. The valvetrain and piston assembly wear at different rates. Although Honda recommends more frequent service intervals, realistically, the average rider who takes care of the bike will get about 50 hours from the piston assembly on a CRF250 and 100 hours from a 450. Valvetrains are a different story. The 250 must be checked for clearance every 4 hours. The estimated life of stock valves is about 40 hours. The 450's titanium intake valves wear quickly, too, and should be replaced with steel parts. The best way to check the condition of the top end is with a leak-down tester. Obvious symptoms of a worn top end include hard starting, sluggish power, popping at idle, and easy to kickstart.

Servicing the top end of a CRF offers a myriad of performance opportunities. Products like high-compression pistons, camshafts, oversized valves or pistons, porting, and multiangle valve jobs can be performed during top end servicing.

Theses are the major components of the top end. This grouping of parts shows some wear. Check the cylinder heads valve seats for pitting or rounding. This cam has flattened and burned spots on the lobes. Examine the valve's sealing surface for cupping. This piston has shiny spots where the valves collided after the chain tensioner failed and allowed the cam to jump. Cylinders wear just below the top surface. Look for dull gray spots that indicate the nickel-composite plating is worn out.

PROJECT 6	How to Rebuild a Top End

Time: 3 hours

Tools: Ratchet and sockets 6, 8, 10, 12, 14 mm, Allen sockets 6, 8, 10 mm, foot-pounds torque wrench, feeler gauge set, needle-nose pliers, small straight-blade screwdriver, number 2 Phillips screwdriver

Talent: ★★★

Tab: $220 and up

Parts: Piston kit $175, gasket kit $45, camshaft $170, Black Diamond valvetrain kit $400

Benefits: Prevent catastrophic engine failure, more power, less vibration and oil consumption

Prepping the Bike for Engine Disassembly

Before you attempt to disassemble the engine, you should remove the seat and fuel tank and pressure-wash the engine and upper frame. This will help prevent dirt from falling into the disassembled engine. Also drain the crankcase oil and coolant. Loosen the carb clamps front and rear, remove the header pipe, and remove the subframe. On the 450 you'll also need to remove the ignition coil and the head-stay brackets. Take care not to discard the thin shim plates mounted to the brackets.

Dots and Triangles

Start by removing the valve cover and the inspection cap from the right-side engine cover. It requires a 10-mm Allen wrench. The cap covers an 8-mm Allen fitting on the end of the crankshaft bolt. Turn the crankshaft clockwise until the dot on the Allen bolt aligns with the triangle embossed on the side cover. The crankshaft is at top dead center (TDC). Observe the camshaft: make sure the lobe points away from the buckets and the dot and triangle marks align under the inspection cap.

Rebuilding your bike's top end gives you the opportunity to replace worn stock parts with new hop-up parts! High-compression pistons give broader power, a big bore beefs up the low end, and Hot Cams can tune the power for either top-end rev or low-end torque.

Check the Valve Clearance First!

Before you disassemble the valvetrain, measure the valve clearance. The valve clearance becomes tighter over time, not looser. When the valves tighten up, they hang open and the edges burn away, causing a lack of

You can quickly access the top end of a CRF by unclamping the carb from the head; removing the header pipe, seat, and tank; then unbolting the top of the subframe and cocking it backward. This will give you enough room to extract the top end in the frame.

compression. If you cannot fit a 0.004-inch/0.10-mm feeler gauge between the cam and bucket or rocker arm, there could be a problem of cupped valves. You can try to install thinner shims to loosen the valve clearance. The general rule on valve wear is this: if you have to install a shim that is three or more sizes smaller than the shim you remove, the valves are worn out.

Disassembling the Top End

The procedure for the 250 and 450 is similar. There are slight differences in the 250 and 450 camshaft sprocket and retainer caps.

Before you disassemble the top end, turn the crankshaft to TDC on the compression stroke and align the dot and triangle located under the 10-mm Allen cap screw on the right-side engine cover.

This is a Motion Pro leak-down pressure tester attached to the spark plug hole. Compressed air of 100 psi is routed through the tester manifold, and a gauge reads the percentage of pressure loss. Leaks can be traced in the intake and exhaust ports for the valve-to-seat problems. Excess pressure escaping though the crankcase vent is a sure sign of a worn-out piston.

A magnifying glass will help you see the wear pattern on the head's valve seat and valve's sealing surface. Cupping or deep pitting means that the valve will have to be replaced and the seat resurfaced at a 45-degree angle.

Leak-Down Testing

A pressure leak-down test is an accurate method of monitoring the condition of the piston and rings, and the valve to seat sealing. The test can be performed quickly if you have the right tools. Motion Pro makes a leak-down testing kit that includes an air pressure regulator and manifold with threaded hoses to fit three different-sized spark plug holes.

A leak-down pressure test begins by cranking the piston up to TDC on the compression stroke. Thread the hose into the spark plug hole and connect it to the pressure manifold. Connect an air pressure source line to the manifold and read the leakage on the gauge in percent. Normal leakage on new engines is 5 to 7 percent. Leakage in the 20 percent and greater range could be worn rings or a bad valve and seat. Pressure leakage can be isolated to its source by listening for leakage in the exhaust pipe or intake air boot that would indicate a bad valve and seat. Worn rings will enable pressure to build up in the crankcase and leak out of the vent tube attached to the top of the valve cover. Once you determine where a leak is, you can do the project that fixes the leak.

Scrub the head and valve seats clean with bathroom cleaner and a soft brass wire brush. Inspect the seats with a magnifying glass.

Use an 8-mm Allen socket and 3/8 ratchets to rotate the crankshaft into position during disassembly or assembly. The crank should always be set to TDC.

Use a thin, straight-blade screwdriver to turn the plunger screw clockwise until it locks in the retracted position. Remove the two mounting bolts and the cam chain tensioner.

1) Insert an 8-mm Allen socket in the right side of the crankshaft and turn the crankshaft clockwise to the TDC position, or when the dot on the crank gear aligns with the triangle on the side cover.

2) Remove the cam chain tensioner cap bolt and insert a thin straight-blade screwdriver in the hole. Turn it clockwise until you feel it click and bottom-out. The tension is now backed off the cam chain, making it easier to disassemble the top end.

3) (450) Loosen and remove the two 6-mm Allen bolts on the sprocket. Use a ratchet, not a hand-impact driver. Don't hold the camshaft using the de-compressor bolt, because you could strip it removing the sprocket bolts. Separate the sprocket

from the chain and let the chain fall into the crankcase where it can easily be retrieved.

4) (250/450) Remove the four 10-mm bolts that retain the camshaft.

5) (250) Take care when removing the camshaft caps, because there are two C-rings and four alignment pins that can fall out and drop into the crankcase. Have a telescopic magnet ready just in case. Slide the left-side cam bearing to the left and pivot the cam downward, so you can separate the chain from the sprocket and remove the cam.

6) (450) Rock the cam cartridge back and forth until the alignment pins break loose from the head. Rock the cartridge up from the intake side and insert two fingers up into the underside of the buckets to prevent them from falling out and dropping the tiny shim pads into the crankcases.

Removing the Head and Cylinder

7) Remove the four head nuts using a 14-mm, six-point socket. Use a long ratchet and some extensions to get enough swing on the ratchet. A telescopic magnet is handy for retrieving the nuts and washers.

8) Remove the three 8-mm hex bolts that hold the head to the cylinder to the crankcases and remove the water spigot in the front of the cylinder.

9) The head and cylinder are fitted with alignment pins, so it may be difficult to remove these parts. Never use a screwdriver or chisel to split the head and cylinder apart, because that will damage the gasket surfaces. Instead, use a dead-shot plastic mallet to split the engine components apart. Remove the head, cylinder, and front chain guide together. This will eliminate the chance of the alignment pins falling into the crankcase.

Cleaning Methods and Supplies

Degrease the cylinder and head with a mineral spirits solvent like PB Blaster or an aqueous solvent. (The ultimate cleaning method that is quickly becoming the standard in cylinder head specialty shops is a baking soda blaster.) Use a Scotch-Brite pad to scrub the burnt oil off the cylinder wall in an X pattern. That will serve to remove the glazing from the crosshatch marks. A stiff nylon brush can be used to safely scrub the combustion chamber and valves. Rinse the parts off and allow them to drip dry.

10) Hot water and strong detergent combined with scrub pads and soft brushes are ideal for gently cleaning top end parts. Take care to dry and lubricate steel parts prone to rusting.

Inspecting

Six main areas of the head need to be inspected. The valves, seats, springs, camshaft, rocker arm, and gasket surface display distinctive wear patterns that help you determine which parts and labor tasks will be needed to recondition the head.

The cylinder head wears most at the seats and guides. Look for pitting and pounding marks on the valve seat with the help of a magnifying glass. Check the guides by extending the valve out about a half-inch and trying to wiggle the valve head. If you feel any movement, the guides are worn.

The best thing about Honda is that the major engine components like cylinders and heads are reasonable to replace. For example, the average aftermarket price for guide and seat replacement with a valve job is double the average mail-order price for a new head.

Unbolt the CRF250 cam caps and take care when removing them; there is a C-clip and alignment pins that can easily fall into the open crankcase.

The Unicam cartridge is susceptible to failure from a lack of oil from loss of oil pressure or volume. This sample cartridge has burnt-on oil from running too hot. Both of the ball bearings are shot and the cam lobes are worn down flatter, which could hurt performance. The rocker arm's roller wears inside and outside. The exhaust lobe contacts the outside and a pin and needle bearing are used inside the roller. If there are any groove lines on the roller face, replace the whole rocker arm assembly.

The titanium intake valves wear in a cup pattern because the valve springs suffer metal fatigue and must be replaced as a set.

Test the cam chain tensioner by trying to depress the plunger. This is especially important on 2002–2003

Clockwise, from top left:

Hold the cylinder with one hand and squeeze the piston rings with your other hand and slowly lower the cylinder down onto the piston assembly evenly. Try rocking the cylinder a little from side to side as you press down on the cylinder.

Clean the head gasket surface, install the two alignment pins, and install the front plastic chain guide before the head gasket.

Install and torque the head nuts in a crisscross pattern. Tighten the three 8-mm bolts last.

Take care when removing the Unicam cartridge. The shims and tappets could fall out; slide your fingers under the intake tappets to support them during removal.

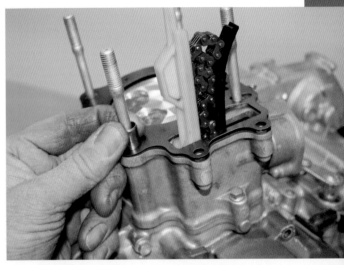

Clockwise from right:

Honda makes a special wedge tool to hold the cam chain tensioner in the retracted position for assembly. You can also use a small screwdriver and thread the plunger in while installing the two mounting bolts.

On the CRF250, you need to slide the left cam bearing toward the sprocket so you can bend the cam down in order to loop the chain on the sprocket.

To fine-tune the camshaft-to-crankshaft alignment, pull a chain link up and roll it in either direction on the sprocket to advance or retard the timing.

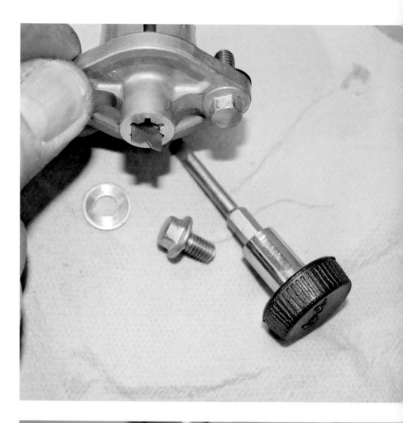

Above: Position the rocker arm shaft with the holes aligned and the bearings in position relative to the C-clips in the caps.

Right: Take care when installing the cam bearing caps, to align the pins and the C-clip at the same time. You can slide the bearings back and forth to get them in the proper position.

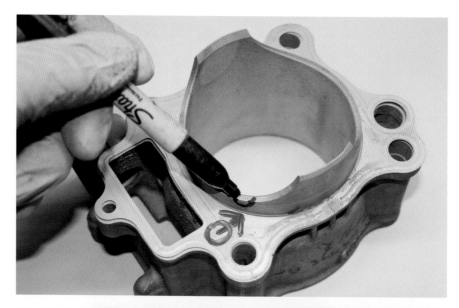

To install a 2005 cylinder on a 2004 CRF250, you have to grind a 3/8-inch relief for clearance of the oil jet. The 2005 and later cylinders have a better skirt design.

Hot Cams makes camshafts for CRFs that enhance the powerband to suit your riding needs.

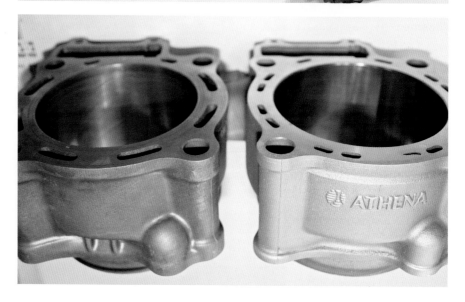

Athena is an Italian company that makes big-bore cylinder kits for CRFs. They make a CRF280 and a CRF490. The cylinders feature deeper water jackets.

PROJECT 8 | How to Install a Black Diamond Valvetrain Kit

Time: 3 hours

Tools: Valve spring compressor, G-clamp or Motion Pro hammer type, tube of fine valve-grinding paste, plunger-stick, tweezers, assembly lube, Scotch-Brite cleaning pad, 10-mm socket or wrench, feeler gauges

Talent: ★★★★

Tab: $425

Parts: Kibblewhite Black Diamond valves and spring kit, head gasket, stem seals, valve shims or Hot Cams shim kit

Benefits: Longer valvetrain life, better sealing, more low-end power, steady power until the rev limiter kicks on

S tart with the cylinder head removed from the engine, clean, and on the bench for breakdown.

1) Use the valve-spring compressor to push down the top retainer, and use a magnet to remove the clips. Take care to separate the clips by intake and exhaust, because on the CRF450 the clips are sized differently.
2) Remove and discard all of the stock valvetrain parts except the clips.
3) Clean the head thoroughly with a Scotch-Brite pad in detergent and hot water. Scrub the valve seats for close inspection.
4) Examine the valve seats for cracks and deep ridges. If the seats are in good condition, you can use fine valve-grinding compound paste to hand-lap the new valves to the seat. Use a plunger stick (auto parts stores) cupped to the valve face and roll it between your hands for a few minutes for each valve. The grinding paste works as a polishing media to help mate the two surfaces flat and smooth for a good seal. Clean the valve and head with brake cleaner and a towel to prepare for assembly.

The Motion Pro valve spring compressor uses a handle with a plunger and magnet. You press on the end of the tool and it compresses the spring and installs the clips.

5) Get a rectangular tray to segment out the valvetrain parts in order for assembly. Separate the parts by exhaust and intake. Place the valves in the order of valve pocket along with the new seals, springs, base washers, top retainers, and clips.

6) Coat each valve stem with moly paste or assembly lube. Assemble each valve and spring set using the valve-spring compressor. A dab of grease and a set of tweezers make it easier to install the clips in the top retainer.

7) Test each valve assembly by tapping on it with a plastic mallet. If the clips are not seated properly in the top retainer, the assembly could spring apart when you tap it with the mallet.

8) The valve clearance will need to be readjusted with shims. Hot Cams sells fairly priced kits with a wide selection of shims for a fraction of the original Honda price.

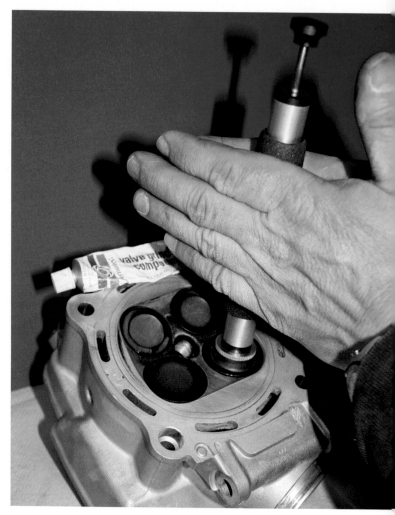

Right: If the valve seats are in good condition, you can hand-lapp finish the stainless steel valves to the seat using a lapping plunger and fine valve grinding compound.

Below: To assemble the valve spring with the Motion Pro tool, start by inserting the clips in the top retainer with a dab of grease to bond them together. Use the tool to press and lock the retainer and clips to the valve.

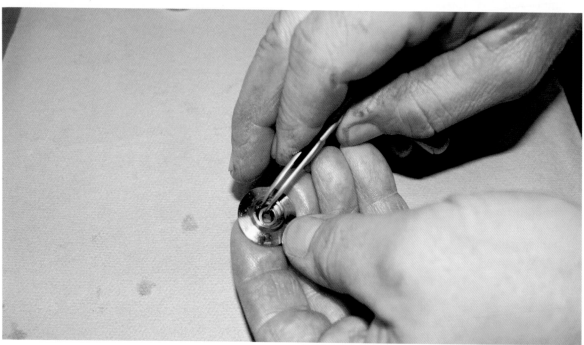

PROJECT 9	Installing a Hot Cam on a CRF450

Time: 2 hours

Tools: Bench vise, snap ring pliers (internal), pick-point, torque wrench, 6-mm Allen socket, 10-mm socket or wrench, Red Loctite, assembly lube, feeler gauges

Talent: ★ ★ ★

Tab: $250

Parts: Hot Cam and Hot Cams shim kit

Benefits: A marked increase in low- to midrange or midrange to top end power

1) Lightly clamp the sprocket-flange side of the camshaft in a bench vise with protective aluminum jaws, to loosen the decompressor bolt and remove the assembly.
2) Loosen and reposition the Unicam cartridge so the left side faces up. Use internal snap ring pliers to remove the ring that retains the left bearing.
3) Wiggle the camshaft to the right while pushing the bearing out the left side. Shift the cam out.
4) Wiggle and shift the new camshaft into position and install the snap ring.
5) Loctite and torque the decompressor bolt to 120 in-lbs, with the cam sprocket-flange lightly clamped in the vise.
6) Set the Unicam cartridge on the head and valve-train, and adjust the shim thickness for a clearance range of 0.004–0.006 inch on the intake valves and 0.009–0.0011 inch on the exhaust valves.

Apply liberal amounts of moly or assembly lube on the camshaft lobes.

New Cam Break-in Tips

The assembly lube will help burnish the cam lobe to the tappet and rocker arm roller. Run the engine with a high idle for 15 minutes and change the oil. The assembly lube eventually contaminates the oil and needs to be flushed.

Top: Hot Cams come in three different profiles. The stage 1 profile gives your engine more low end and mid-range. The stage 2 profile adds to your engine's mid-range to top end output, and stage 3 is designed for big-bore kits only.

Right: You can loosen the cam sprocket bolts and decompressor bolt with a 6-mm Allen socket.

Above: To loosen the auto-decompressor bolt, clamp the cam sprocket in a bench vise equipped with a set of soft aluminum jaws.

Left: Use internal snap ring pliers to remove the clip.

Below: Slide the bearing out the right side so the cam can be removed.

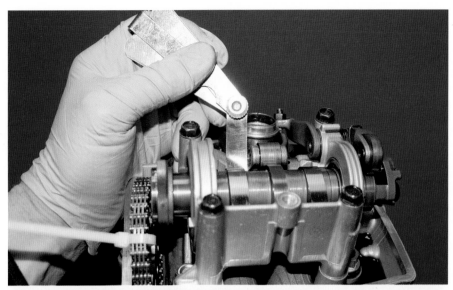

Check the valve clearance. Hot Cam recommends setting the clearance on the tight side of the spec.

With the crankshaft at TDC, the sprocket should be in this position, with the cam lobes facing the intake side of the head. Looking through the holes in the sprocket, look for alignment of the triangle and the straight lines of the sprocket.

Coat the cam lobes with moly paste as an assembly lube. Run the engine for 15 minutes at a high idle and change the crankcase oil. That is all you need to do to break in a new Hot Cam.

Chapter 5
BOTTOM END REBUILDING

Projects 10–11

Rebuilding the bottom end of a four-stroke engine is easier than a two-stroke. There are fewer special tools needed and the crank just drops in without any special knowledge or techniques. Of course, the cam-to-crank timing is a bit tricky, but we cover that subject in depth in the top end rebuilding chapter.

The toughest thing about rebuilding the bottom end is paying attention to detail and looking for potential trouble signs before they cause your engine's "energetic disassembly." This chapter will show you the ins and outs of bottom end rebuilding.

- Rebuilding the Bottom End with a Hot Rod Crank and Bearing Kit

- Installing a Baja Designs Wide-Ratio Transmission Kit

PROJECT 10

Rebuilding the Bottom End with a Hot Rod Crank and Bearing Kit

---

Time: 3 hours

Tools: Ratchet and sockets 8, 10, 12, 14, 17, 19, and 27 mm, Allen sockets 6, 8, and 10 mm, snap ring pliers, pneumatic or electric impact wrench, inch- and foot-pounds torque wrenches, gasket scraper, wooden box, parts washer, Motion Pro clutch hub holder, dead-shot plastic mallet, flat chisel, Honda special tools: gear holder number 07724-001A200, spanner nut socket number 07716-0020100, flywheel puller number 07933-1480000

Talent: ★★★★★

Tab: $500

Parts: Moose Racing gasket/seal kit $100, Hot Rod crankshaft $300, Hot Rod main bearing set $100

Benefits: Renewed engine life and better overall performance

Engine Hygiene

Mineral spirits solvents like PB Blaster parts cleaner are essential to breaking down the oil film that coats the engine parts. You can buy a 5-gallon container from most auto parts stores, even a bench-top parts washer that includes a pump and brush to facilitate cleaning. You need to get the oil film off of the parts in order to facilitate the removal and installation of new bearings and seals. Place the engine on a wooden-framed box of 2x4s so you can support the engine during disassembly and assembly.

Clutch Disassembly and Inspection

If the clutch assembly is in good condition, try to remove it as a set. Start by removing the six bolts and springs on the pressure plate; remove the actuator assembly, paying close attention to the shim placement

The left side of the crankshaft has an oil jet that will be ruined with conventional flywheel pullers. The Honda tool comes with a protective cap for the crank that is installed before removing the flywheel.

and order of the thrust bearing. Slide out the pushrod and fold down the retaining washer on the big center nut that holds the clutch on the main shaft.

Shifter, Kickstarter, Balancer, and Primary Gear Disassembly Removal

You will have to remove the shift shaft, kick-starter cartridge, and the spanner nut and bolt that retain the balancer and primary gears. The best way to remove the primary-gear bolt is with a pneumatic or electric impact wrench. There is a factory holding tool for these gears; it looks like a wedge of a gear and fits between the primary and balancer gears. There is also a special spanner socket for the balancer gear nut listed in the legend above. The shift drum can remain in the cases during rebuilding.

Splitting the Crankcases

Remove all the case bolts, including the hidden one on CRF450s located under the sump tube. You don't need

Honda sells a special spanner socket and gear-wedge tools for holding and removing the balancer. You can improvise on the holding tool, but the spanner socket is a Honda special tool and only available from dealers.

53

Starting with a clean case half, put the bearings in the freezer for two hours then heat the main bearing pocket with a heat gun for about three minutes before installation.

a crankcase-splitting tool on a CRF like the CR models use. You should be able to use a dead-shot plastic mallet to tap around the outside of the cases while suspending the engine a few inches over the box so most of the engine's weight is used to help separate the cases. This will help break the bond of the case alignment pins. If the cases start to split apart with an uneven gap from front to rear, then tap on the right-side crankcase with a plastic mallet. You may also have to tap on the countershaft, but be careful not to break the bearing support ring that is cast into the case.

You don't need to remove the transmission in order to change the crankshaft and main bearings if the gears and shift forks are in good shape. The best way to keep the gears and shims on the transmission shafts is with rubber bands or wire.

Transmission Disassembly and Inspection

To remove the transmission shafts, you need to first remove the shift forks. There are three shift forks in the transmission, and they are marked "L" for left, "C" for center, and "R" for right. Pull the rods that hold the

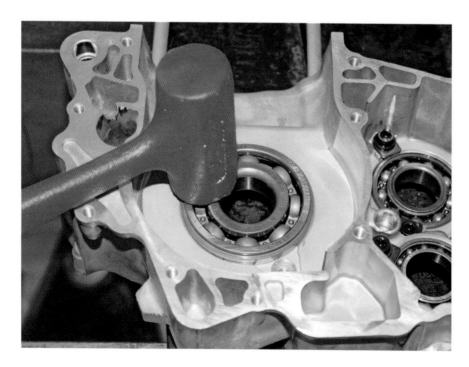

Set the main bearing in the pocket and use a plastic mallet to hammer on the outer race until the bearing is deep enough for the bearing clips to be fully tightened.

forks, and then pull out the forks. Place the forks onto the rods, and set them in a parts bin in the order that they fit into the engine. They each have a different radius, so you can't install them in the wrong position. Visually check the sides of the shift forks for blue marks. That would indicate that the forks are bent and need to be replaced. Remove the transmission shafts, paying close attention to the placement of shims on the ends of the transmission shafts; sometimes they will stick to the bearings and fall out later when you are washing the cases. Visually inspect the gear engagement dogs for wear. If they are worn, the female and male dogs will have shiny spots on the corners. Also, the bike will have the tendency to jump out of gear during acceleration. If you are installing new Honda replacement transmission parts or a Baja Designs wide-ratio kit, skip to that section of this chapter for more information.

Crankshaft Removal and Inspection

Sometimes, the crank will be difficult to remove from the right-side main bearing. Never strike the end of the crank will a metal hammer; try a plastic mallet first. If that doesn't work, then thread the primary-gear nut on to protect the threads and use a hydraulic press to remove the crank.

Set the crankshaft and transmission in the right case. Make sure that the crank and trans shafts rotate smoothly. Turn the shift drum while turning the countershaft and shift it through the gears.

Bearing Removal and Installation

The best way to remove or install bearings is by heating the aluminum crankcases with a propane torch, and then using a hydraulic press to gently push them out. Never pound the bearings out with a hammer and punch. The outer race of the bearing is the only part of the bearing where a press slug should be placed. Large sockets or discs work as well as press slugs. Placing the new bearings in the freezer for two hours and heating the cases with the torch will enable you to install the bearings without a press. Fit the bearings into position with as little stress as possible exerted on the crank ends.

Crankshaft Installation

CRFs use ball bearings in the right-side case to support the crankshaft, and there is a slight press fit of the crankshaft into the bearing. Here is a simple way to

If you have a hydraulic press, press each bearing down until it bottoms in the pocket, with only a tiny part of the bearing exposed above the case.

install the crankshaft into the right case. Place the crank in a freezer for two hours so it contracts in size. Get a cylindrical piece of aluminum with the same diameter as the inner bearing race. Heat and expand the bearing's inner race by heating the aluminum slug with a propane torch for five minutes while it rests on the inner race of the right-side main bearing. Drop the cold crank into the hot right main bearing.

Assembling the Crankcases

With the crank and transmission fitted into the right crankcase, you're ready to assemble the cases. Place the center case gasket on the alignment pins. Position the left case over the crank and transmission shafts while using an index card to hold the oil pump upside down. The left-side case on a CRF uses a roller bearing, so the case should just slide together easily. If it doesn't, there is something binding between the transmission shafts—check to see that they are firmly seated. Install the bolts that fasten the cases together. You may need to tap the case lightly because you are trying to align eight different cylindrical pieces all together (crank, transmission shafts, shift-fork rods, shift drum, and case alignment pins). Once the case bolts are hand-tight, try to turn the crankshaft and the transmission shafts. The transmission should turn easily, and the crankshaft should turn with some resistance. Tighten the case bolts in two stages of torque and use an inch/pounds torque wrench to 100 in-lbs.

Bench Testing

When you get the lower end together and the cases are sealed tight, install the shifting mechanism and turn the clutch shaft while clicking through the gears. The transmission is your main consideration when bench testing. Make sure that the shafts turn and shift the transmission through from first to fifth. If they don't turn or shift smoothly, something is binding in the transmission. You'll need to slit the cases and check that the shafts and rods are firmly seated in the right case half.

Final Assembly

Assemble the rest of the engine components, mount the engine in the frame, and connect all of the electrical wires, control cables, and linkages. Torque all the mounting bolts, and then you're ready to break in your rebuilt engine.

Breaking in a New Bottom End

The new lower end will need some patient break-in time. The best way is to ride the bike easy for three separate 10-minute sessions with a 20-minute rest period between sessions. Change the crankcase oil after the final break-in session, because the assembly lube will have mixed with the oil and performed its job by then.

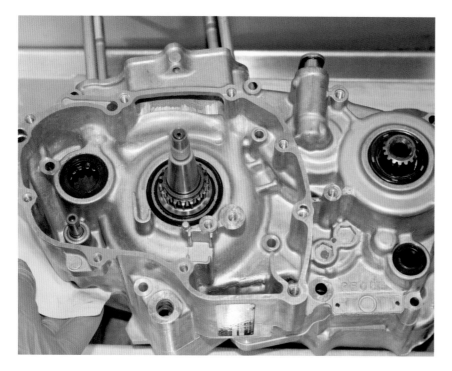

The final step to prepare the engine for assembly is to insert the oil pump in the left case half and hold it in place with a thin plastic card, while you install it onto the right side where all the components are fitted.

PROJECT 11	Installing a Baja Designs Wide-Ratio Transmission Kit

Time: 1 hour extra during bottom end rebuilding

Tools: Hand grinder and tool bits for steel and aluminum, snap ring pliers, bench vise, aluminum jaws

Talent: ★★★★★

Tab: $650

Parts: Baja Designs Kit, Honda snap rings part number 90602-259-010 (four pieces)

Benefits: More top speed from the top three gears

1) With the transmission removed from the engine, lightly clamp the main and countershafts in a vise with soft aluminum jaws.
2) Use snap ring pliers to remove the snap rings and disassemble the gears in order, laying them out on a clean, flat surface.
3) Set the corresponding Baja wide-ratio gears next to the original Honda gears, paying strict attention to the positions of the shims and snap rings. A note on snap rings: they are stamped from spring steel so one edge is rounded and the opposite edge is sharp. The direction of force applied by the gear should face the sharp edge. Never reuse snap rings. Always replace them with Honda parts, not generic snap rings.
4) Install the gears, shims, and snap rings in order. The Baja Designs instruction sheet has an excellent drawing of the gears and order of installation.
5) In order to use wide-ratio gears, the crankcases and shift forks must be ground down for additional clearance. Use the template provided in the kit.

The marks area shows the effective area that must be ground for clearance to the new larger gears.

The Baja Designs wide ratio gears set next to the gears they will replace. Buy new Honda snap rings because they aren't reuseable.

Chapter 6
CLUTCH AND DRIVETRAIN

Projects 12–14

- Troubleshooting Worn Clutch Parts
- How to Install an Aftermarket Performance Clutch Kit
- Changing to a Rekluse Z-Start Auto Clutch
- Installing a Magura Hydraulic Clutch Kit

A clutch is a mechanical device that provides a controllable link between the crankshaft and transmission. A CRF clutch consists of a clutch basket, inner hub, pressure plate, pushrod actuating mechanism, several fiber drive plates, a matching set of metallic driven plates, and springs. The clutch basket is fastened to the primary driven gear with rivets and cushioned with rubber dampers. The basket has channels to contain the fiber drive plates, and those channels develop wear marks with use. The inner hub is fastened to the main shaft of the transmission and splined to hold the metallic driven plates. The pressure plate controls the spring pressure and friction exerted to the fiber and metallic plates. The actuating mechanism provides a link from the hand lever to the pressure plate. The clutch plates, backed by the springs, act as the friction link between the engine and transmission.

CRFs use cheap cast aluminum for the clutch basket, hub, and pressure plate. These parts last about 100 hours on a CRF450 and about 40 hours on a CRF250. The more you fan the clutch, the faster the stock parts wear out. Most pro racers change the entire clutch assembly on CRF250s with a Hinson Racing Pro Kit that includes a billet aluminum, Teflon-coated basket, hub, and ribbed pressure plate.

Troubleshooting Worn Clutch Parts

The typical problems of a CRF clutch include slipping, jerky action, dragging, and grinding noises. Slipping occurs because the plates and springs are worn out. Jerky action and dragging occur when the clutch basket, inner hub, or pressure plate develop deep wear marks. Grinding noises occur when the needle bearing and bushing that support the clutch basket wear out. You can visually check the clutch parts in the following ways:

Check the fiber plates for cracks and wear between the raised and lowered sections. The metallic plates will be blue or brown in color when they get overheated from chronic slippage. Check the clutch basket for deep grooves on the channels where the drive-plate tabs slide. A bit of axial flex between the clutch basket and the primary gear is normal, because the two parts are engaged on several rubber bushings. But if you discover rubber blobs in the transmission oil, then the clutch basket needs to be replaced. If the clutch basket is worn, you also need to check the inner clutch hub. The sliding motion of the driven plates' teeth wears the splines of the inner hub. Sometimes you can polish down the high spots, but if the marks are really deep, it will have to be replaced. Examine the pressure plate for an obvious edge at the engagement surface.

Above: Top racers use Hinson Racing clutches. This one was autographed by Jeremy McGrath.

Right: Honda clutch baskets are made of soft cast aluminum. When the fingers of the basket are grooved deep like this one, the clutch will drag.

Below: This is a side view of the clutch components. Starting from left to right are the clutch basket, inner hub, plates, and pressure plate.

PROJECT 12

How to Install an Aftermarket Performance Clutch Kit

Time: 2 hours

Tools: Ratchet and sockets 3, 4, 8, 10, 12, 27 mm, Allen socket 8 mm, pneumatic or electric impact wrench, drill, 1/4-inch drill bit, flat-blade screwdriver, propane torch or heat gun, arbor or hydraulic press, Red Loctite, center punch

Talent: ★ ★ ★

Tab: $165–$575

Parts: Aftermarket basket, hub, and pressure plate

Benefits: Better clutch action, less oil contamination, longer clutch-plate life

Five aftermarket manufacturers offer replacement clutch baskets: Barnett, Hinson, Moose, Vortex, and Wiseco. Most of these products are machined from billet aluminum and hard-anodized for wear resistance. Barnett clutch baskets feature steel inserts for the drive-plate channels. Hinson products are hard-anodized and coated with Teflon to reduce friction. Hinson offers replacement rubber bushings because they tend to wear out on 250-cc bikes. Hinson

also offers a wider variety of performance clutch parts like inner hubs, pressure plates, and hard-anodized aluminum driven plates that are lightweight with a rough surface finish for more friction. Wiseco clutch baskets are forged from billet slugs and are lighter than all the other baskets. Wiseco also makes heavy-duty pressure plates that resist flexing.

All of the aftermarket clutch baskets require you to remove the original primary gear, kick-start gear, and rubber bushings from your clutch basket.

Here is an overview of how to install any aftermarket clutch basket.

1) Drain the gearbox oil and coolant from the engine. Bottle these fluids separately. Most municipal garages and auto dealers accept small amounts of coolant and oil for recycling.
2) Remove the kick-start lever, brake lever, coolant hose, and engine guards. Remove the right-side engine cover—take care to look for the alignment pins between the case and cover—and the thrust washer on the kick-starter cartridge.
3) Remove the clutch spring retaining bolts, springs, pressure plate, and actuating mechanism. Check the springs for proper free length; look for a deep edge on the pressure plate that would indicate too much wear. Examine the actuating mechanism for galling or broken radial bearings.
4) This next step, removing the clutch hub-retaining nut, is fairly difficult, and there are different

Drain the transmission oil and coolant, lean the bike on the left side and remove the kick-starter, rear brake lever, and the right-side engine cover.

PROJECT 14 | Installing a Magura Hydraulic Clutch Kit

Time: 15 minutes

Tools: Ratchet and 8-mm socket, pliers

Talent: ★

Tab: $300

Parts: Magura Hydraulic Clutch Kit

Benefits: Easier clutch pulling, less forearm pump

Based on my description, riders can make a determination if an auto clutch is right for them. Additionally, the magazines have written at length about the pros and cons of an auto clutch. I'm just giving a short overview of what's involved in changing to an auto clutch before riders actually buy one and read the instructions.

1) Remove the clutch cable and lever assembly.

2) Attach the Magura hydraulic clutch lever to the handlebars.

3) Attach the Magura cable to the actuating lever in the case and fold over the clip to retain the cable end.

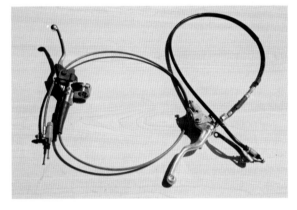

Here are the original cable parts next to the Magura hydraulic components.

Fold over the cable-mounting bracket to fit the Magura actuator.

Use pliers to squeeze tight the cable end.

65

Chapter 7
COOLING SYSTEM

- Basic Maintenance Tips
- Installing a Boyesen High-Flow Water Pump Kit

- Upgrading Cooling Capacity with Fluidyne Radiators and CV4 Silicon Hoses

The cooling system dissipates some of the heat energy from combustion. Heat transfers into the water jackets of the cylinder and head. The coolant in the water jackets is a mixture of distilled water and glycol. The water pump is gear-driven by the crankshaft, spinning an impeller that circulates the coolant through the water pipes, hoses, and radiators. The radiators are heat exchangers, allowing airflow to carry away heat energy as the coolant flows through the finned aluminum channels of the radiator.

The stock CRFs have adequate cooling systems but some riding situations, like riding through tight woods or mountain climbing, where the engine load is high and the air flow past the radiators is low, can strain the system. As normal wear and crash damage occurs to your bike, you may consider improvements to the system with performance parts. Boyesen makes water pump covers and impellers that produce greater flow. Fluidyne makes oversized radiators with heavy-duty side brackets. High-pressure radiator caps and brands of coolant can also offer minor gains in performance, but sometimes the best improvements can be had from simple, basic maintenance.

Cooling System 101

Understanding how the cooling system components work together is key to learning how to service and improve your CRF.

Components of the Cooling System

Bearing: One ball bearing supports the water pump shaft in the right-side cover.

Cap: The cap is fitted to the top of the radiator.

Coolant: A mixture of water and glycol designed to increase the temperature range of the coolant.

Impeller: The impeller is a rotary fan that pumps the coolant.

Radiator: A liquid-to-air heat exchanger.

Seals: There are two seals in a water pump, one for sealing coolant, the other for sealing oil.

Water jackets: The hollow cavities cast into the cylinder and head, through which the coolant flows.

Water pump: The water pump consists of a housing with fittings, shaft, bearings, seals, and impeller.

Water Wetter: Water Wetter is an organic chemical that breaks down the surface tension of water. Common wetting agents include aspartame, the same chemical used as an artificial sweetener.

Basic Maintenance Tips

Check it!

CRFs aren't equipped with warning lights or gauges to indicate the loss of coolant or flow, so its best to check the coolant level, color, and flow every few engine hours. Check the level and color with the engine off and when it's cold. The proper level is just above the inner radiator cores. If the level is too high, expansion and flow can cause the cap's plunger to fail and auto-siphon the coolant out the vent hose. Look for oil floating in the top of the still radiator. That can indicate a leak between the transmission-side seal in the water pump. Occasionally, the radiator cap can fail, but they are easily checked with a special tool that consists of a pressure pump and a cylinder to which the cap attaches. Most motorcycle and automotive repair shops have this tool and only charge a small fee to test caps.

Cap it!

The radiator cap is spring-loaded, and if the pressure and temperature reach a certain point, a plunger overcomes the spring and coolant flows out the vent tube to prevent the hoses from bursting. Caps are available in different spring pressure ratings. A radiator cap with a pressure rating of 20 psi, as opposed to the stock 14 psi, will allow for a higher operating temperature before the coolant boils and overcomes the spring pressure of the plunger in the cap.

Flush it!

Radiators need to be flushed annually because the interaction of coolant and aluminum produces a white, flaky corrosion that eventually clogs the radiator cores. Tap water has all sorts of minerals and salt that can cause corrosion of the aluminum parts. The best mixture of coolant for temperatures above freezing is distilled water and a small amount of wetting agent. If you are going to operate your bike in a wide temperature range, just use a 50/50 mixture of antifreeze and distilled water.

Wet it!

Water Wetter is a surfactant that breaks down the surface tension of water. This is important on a CRF, because microboiling in the water jackets is a significant problem. Microboiling occurs because the surfaces in the water jackets of the cylinder and head are roughcast. The rapidly circulating coolant can't conform to the rough surface, considering the surface tension of water. If you get the engine up to operating temperature, then stop riding while keeping the engine running, eventually the coolant will boil and blow the radiator cap. As I mentioned above, Water Wetter is made of aspartame, an artificial sweetener. A mixture of distilled water and aspartame will transfer more BTUs of heat than any popularly marketed motorcycle coolant product.

Troubleshooting Tips

Here is a list of the typical coolant system problems, with corresponding causes and action suggestions for fixing the problems.

Problem: Coolant overflows out of the hose located under the radiator cap.
Cause: Radiator cap faulty, or the coolant level is too high.
Action Suggestion: Pressure test the cap and lower the coolant level to just above the cores.

Problem: Coolant overflows out of the hose located under the radiator cap.
Cause: Water pump impeller stripped from the shaft.
Action Suggestion: Check impeller by observing flow just under the radiator cap with the engine idling. The fluid should circulate rapidly with an increase in engine rpm.

Problem: Coolant overflows out of the hose located under the radiator cap.
Cause: Head gasket is blown, allowing high-pressure combustion gases to enter the water jackets.
Action Suggestion: Replace the head gasket and lap-flat the sealing surfaces of the head and cylinder to remove the warpage.

Problem: Coolant dribbles out of the bottom of the water pump cover through a tiny hole.
Cause: The water pump shaft, bearings, and seals are worn out. The tiny hole at the bottom of the water pump housing is located between the two seals and is designed to channel the leaking coolant away from the transmission.
Action Suggestion: Replace the water pump shaft, bearing, and both seals (all the parts will be worn).

PROJECT 15	Installing a Boyesen High-Flow Water Pump Kit

Time: 30 minutes

Tools: Ratchet and sockets 8, 10, 12, 17 mm, Allen socket 8 mm, plastic mallet, Phillips and straight-blade screwdrivers

Talent: ★

Tab: $160

Parts: Honda water pump components, Boyesen impeller, gaskets, coolant

Benefit: Lower coolant temperature, greater engine life

The CRF450 has chronic water-pump problems. The water pump is driven directly off the end of the crankshaft, instead of through a reduction gear. The CRF450 only uses one bearing instead of two, like a traditional gear-driven pump, so there is less support for the shaft. Direct-driven water pumps reduce the space requirements with a slight sacrifice in reliability. The CRF250 uses a gear-driven pump, and the shaft is supported by two bearings, one in the side cover and

the other in the case. It is more reliable than the CRF450 design. All late-model, four-stroke dirt bikes use a weep hole located in a cavity between the oil and water seals. If one of the seals leaks, the fluid (either oil or coolant) will leak out of the weep hole to indicate that the water pump needs servicing. Mixing of the oil and coolant on a four-stroke engine can cause catastrophic damage, which is why the weep-hole-type designs were invented. To check the condition of your

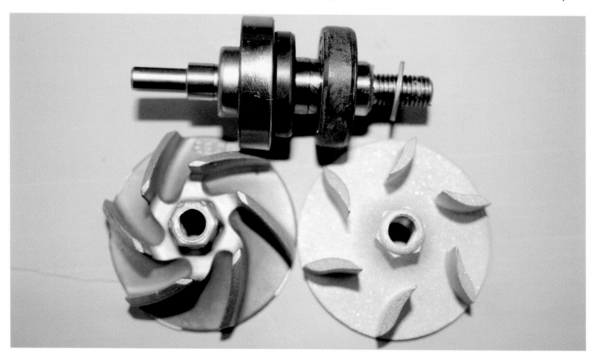

The Boyesen high-flow impeller (right) has a patented nautilus shape to improve the water pump's efficiency.

CRF's water pump, start by cleaning and unplugging the weep hole of debris such as dried-on mud. Start the engine and rev it in neutral. Look at the weep hole and look for droplets of coolant.

Boyesen Engineering invented and patented a unique, high-volume, water-pump impeller featuring a Nautilus-style blade design that greatly improves hydrodynamic efficiency and lowers coolant temperatures.

If you are planning on installing the Boyesen high-flow impeller, you should replace these parts at the same time: water-pump shaft, water seal, oil seal, bearing, and copper washer. The cost of these Honda parts is about $95 for the CRF250 and $75 for the CRF450.

Radiator hoses don't just pull off once you remove the clamp. Use hose pliers to turn the hose to break it loose before removing it from the fitting.

Honda radiators are prone to bending when dropped on their sides—the core could shift and break, causing a dangerous hot leak. Fluidyne radiators have thick side plates to resist bending.

This water pump got clogged from a chemical reaction between softened tap water and aluminum. Use only premixed coolant or distilled water with water wetter.

With the side cover removed, you can put a wrench
on the shaft to tighten it.

If all you're changing is the impeller, just drain the coolant, remove the pump cover, and unthread the
10-mm bolt on the impeller to swap it with the Boyesen part.

Step-by-Step Water Pump Rebuilding

All of the old parts are stripped out and replaced for rebuilding of the water pump. The bearings can be hammered out with a deep well socket and a plastic dead-shot mallet.

The water pump is easy to rebuild. Installing the Boyesen impeller is just a matter of threading it onto the water pump shaft.

1) Start by draining the transmission oil and the coolant. Unthread the rear brake pedal bolt and the kick-starter bolts. Remove the kick-start lever and fold the brake pedal to the side so you can remove the right-side cover bolts.

2) Remove the four bolts from the water pump cover and move it out of the way. Before you remove the right-side engine cover, unthread the impeller by turning the 10-mm nut counterclockwise.

3) Remove the right-side engine cover and set it on a bench to remove the water pump components. With the impeller and copper washer removed, slide the shaft out toward the engine side. Use a screwdriver to pry out the water seal, and then use a 12-mm socket and mallet to drive out the oil seal and bearing. Clean the water pump shaft cavity with brake cleaner to remove any oil, grease, and coolant before installing the new parts.

4) Use a 17-mm socket to drive in the bearing flush to the cover edge. Before installing the seals, apply a dab of grease under the seal lip and install the oil seal with the spring-band side of the seal facing toward the bearing. Install the water seal with the spring band facing out toward the impeller. It is very important that the spring band faces the pressure side of the fluid, or the water pump will leak coolant or oil from the weep hole.

5) Slide a new copper washer on the shaft and thread on the new Boyesen impeller. Use a 10-mm socket on the impeller and a 14-mm open-end wrench to hold the shaft from the engine side. Torque the impeller to 90 in-lbs, or hand-tight. Take care not to strip the threads of your expensive new impeller! Now you can reinstall the right-side engine cover using a new gasket.

Honda Part Numbers for Water Pump Components

CRF250
Shaft 19240-KRN-670
Water seal 91211-KRN-671
Oil seal 91201-148-003
Bearing 91001-KA4-003
Copper washer 90447-KE1-000
Right-side cover gasket 15650-KRN-670

CRF450
Shaft 19241-MEB-670
Water seal 91211-KA3-761
Oil seal 91201-965-000
Bearing 91001-KA4-003
Copper washer 90447-KE1-000
Right-side cover gasket 11394-MEB-670

COOLING SYSTEM

PROJECT 16

Upgrading the Cooling Capacity with Fluidyne Radiators and CV4 Silicon Hoses

Time: 1 hour

Tools: Ratchet and sockets 6, 8, and 10 mm, hose pliers

Talent: ★

Tab: $650

Parts: Fluidyne radiators, CV4 hoses, and coolant

Benefit: Lower coolant temperature, greater engine life, better protection from coolant system punctures

The stock Honda radiators are prone to clogging when tap water is used instead of distilled water. The radiators are also structurally weak, so even minor side crashes can tweak the tanks-to-cores alignment. Installing a set of CRD heavy-duty, crush-proof radiator guards will help, but these are still cheap radiators with a limited lifespan.

Fluidyne is a company with a strong heritage in NASCAR and SCORE truck racing. They specialize in making heavy-duty, thermally efficient radiators with higher-volume tanks and greater core surface area. Fluidyne radiators also feature a 16-pound cap, which is greater than OEM radiators. Another important benefit for off-road riders is that the thick side panels

Fluidyne radiators are available with colored CV4 silicon hoses available in blue and red.

are welded to the tanks, making them structurally stronger than Honda radiators. The inside areas of the cores are wider, which reduces the chance of clogging if tap water is inadvertently used with antifreeze.

CV4 makes puncture-proof silicon hoses that are molded to the same shape as the original Honda hoses. CV4 hoses are also available in complementary colors, like red and blue. If you are considering switching over to Fluidyne radiators, then you should consider ordering the hose set, too. The main reason is that it's unlikely you'll be able to remove all of the original hoses from the radiator spigots without puncturing at least some of them. If your original radiators are not completely destroyed, you can probably sell them as a set on eBay to offset the cost of the Fluidyne/CV4 replacements. Considering that the aftermarket parts are less expensive than the OEM Honda parts, choosing Fluidyne radiators is an easy choice when the cooling system needs serious maintenance. Here is the procedure for installing Fluidyne radiators and a CV4 hose set.

1) Start by removing the seat, fuel tank, and radiator scoops. Drain the coolant into a sealed plastic container and dispose of it at an automotive repair shop. A shop will probably charge about $1 per quart of coolant, because they have to pay a recycling company to recover this toxic fluid.

2) Spray all of the hose clamps with penetrating oil to make it easy to unthread the bolts without stripping the clamp threads. Remove the hose clamps, louvers, mounting bolts, captured nuts, and rubber grommets from the original radiators. Check the quality of the original parts and replace them if they are damaged.

Install the rubber grommets and captured nuts to the new radiators and mount them onto the bike.

3) Install the clamps on the hoses and slide them to the middle of the hoses. Install the hoses on the spigots and tighten the clamps. Honda clamps have a 6-mm hex bolt and Phillips screw head. You will have a tendency to overtighten the 6-mm bolts, but you are unlikely to have a strong enough grip to strip the clamp threads using a screwdriver. If you strip any of the clamps, replace them with the stainless steel type available from most auto parts stores.

4) Fill the radiators with a mixture of distilled water and antifreeze or a premixed coolant product, and check for leaks. Start the engine and look for leaks. If there is a leak, try tightening the clamps. Check the coolant level after a few minutes, because air pockets may have been trapped in the cores, showing a false coolant level when you initially filled the radiators.

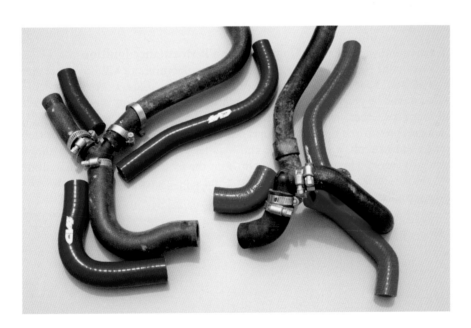

Remove the left and right hose sets from the bike and place the new hoses next to the old hoses then remove and replace them one at a time to avoid mixing them up. Pay attention to the orientation of the hoses but don't tighten them until they are mounted on the bike.

Chapter 8
ELECTRICAL SYSTEM

- Performing an Electrical System Checkup
- Installing an Electrex Lighting Kit
- Upgrading to a Performance Ignition
- Installing a Flywheel Weight

Performing an Electrical System Checkup

Troubleshooting electrical systems is divided into the obvious and the mysterious. Performing a systems check starts with looking for obvious problems like dirty connectors, burned wires, faulty kill switch, broken plug cap, fouled plug, and coils with rusted grounds. Pull the wire connectors apart and spray them clean with electrical contact cleaner. After the connectors dry, inject a bit of dielectric grease in the connector spades to prevent corrosion.

One not-so-obvious cause of no-spark specific to CRF models is the short-circuiting of the signal coil located under the left-side cover. The soldered connectors are uncoated. If metal particles are produced in the crankcases, the particles will adhere to the coil's two contacts and short-circuit the ignition. The connectors can be coated with JB Weld epoxy.

The most common electrical problems with CRFs are a lack of spark plug maintenance and water that gets forced under the plug cap. Look on the right side of the cylinder head; there is a small hole. That is the spark plug cavity's drain hole. That should be plugged with a golf tee before you wash your bike. Otherwise, water flows through the hole and gets pressurized up under the spark plug cap, causing a short circuit. It is critical that the spark plug is changed every 20 hours on a CRF, because the electrode starts to deteriorate. That places a greater load on the secondary coil and

igniter box, which can eventually lead to an expensive replacement repair.

Testing the Black Box

The black box located under the front number plate accepts AC voltage generated by the flywheel magnet and stator coils. It then converts and amplifies the voltage into DC, sets the ignition timing, and sends the power to the secondary coil to be discharged across the spark plug gap to ground. Honda outlines some simple resistance and voltage tests in the factory service manual. But these tests can only give an indication if the black box is capable of completing a circuit. The tests cannot evaluate a faulty ignition map. The only way to determine if the black box has a faulty ignition map is by substituting a new box and test riding the bike for smooth roll-on performance.

Upgrading to a Performance Ignition

There are two manufacturers of CRF performance ignition products on the market: Vortex and Pro Circuit. The aftermarket ignition modules replace the original black box. The Pro Circuit ignition is preprogrammed, and the Vortex has a 10-position clicker and handlebar-mounted button that allows you to switch on the fly to a less-aggressive ignition map for starts and slippery traction conditions.

Dielectric grease should be applied to the metal connectors to seal water out and prevent corrosion.

Pro Circuit makes rev boxes for the CRF250 and 450.

PROJECT 17 | Installing an Electrex Lighting Coil Kit

Time: 1 hour

Tools: Ratchet and 8-mm socket, hand-impact driver with number 1 and number 2 Phillips screwdriver bits, hammer, dead-shot plastic mallet, propane torch or heat gun

Talent: ★ ★ ★

Tab: Electrex Lighting coils $230, Moose Racing wiring kit with switch and AC voltage regulator $80, aftermarket headlight and taillight kits from Acerbis, Baja Designs, Dakar, or UFO $100–$520, hydraulic brake light switch $20

Parts: Electrex Lighting Coil Kit, Baja Designs Dual-Sport Kit or individual UFO headlight and taillight, Moose Racing wiring switch kit and voltage limiter, left-side engine cover gasket, electrical tape

Benefits: Makes a CRF enduro legal

Electrex makes a complete stator plate that gives you the extra power to run lights, in addition to the standard ignition generator and signal coils. Wire connectors to run AC lights are already part of the wiring loom. To install the Electrex stator plate you'll need a left-side engine-cover gasket. Start by removing the seat and gas tank, and unplug the wire connectors on the top right side of the frame. Use a small, straight-blade screwdriver to depress the connector lock before you pull the connectors apart. On the engine, remove the left-side engine cover and clean out the oil before attempting to remove the stator plate. Set the cover firmly on a bench and use a hand-impact driver with a number 2 Phillips socket to remove the stator plate's mounting screws. Pull the entire stator plate and wiring loom and replace it with the Electrex unit. Apply a dab of Blue Loctite to the Phillips screws and tighten them with a hand-impact driver.

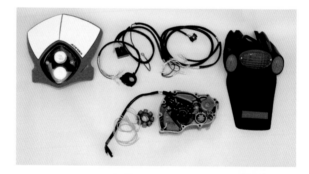

Above Right: Companies like UFO and Acerbis make clip-on headlights and taillights. Electrex makes lighting coil kits that just bolt on. Moose Racing makes a wire loom, switch, and regulator kit, to link the coils and lights.

Right: Use an electric or pneumatic impact wrench to remove the flywheel nut.

Use a Honda flywheel puller with protective end cap, to extract the flywheel for modifications.

1) Drain the crankcase oil, and remove the shift lever and the bolts that retain the left-side engine cover.
2) Pull off the side cover, disconnect the generator wires, and clean the oil residue from the cover.
3) Heat the three number 1 Phillips screws in order to break the bond of the thread locking agent. Use a hand-impact driver to loosen and remove the screws. Install the new Electrex lighting coil ring.
4) Apply Blue Loctite to the three mounting screws and tighten them with the hand-impact driver.
5) Reinstall the left-side cover with a new gasket.
6) Connect the wires and thread in the Moose Racing wire loom and voltage regulator. Mount the handlebar switch on the left side of the bars and the voltage regulator to a convenient place on the frame. You'll need to drill a small hole in the frame to mount the regulator.
7) Mount the headlight and taillight assemblies and make wire connectors if needed.

Barely Street Legal

For events like enduros and dual-sport rides that use rural roads, you'll need head, tail, and brake lights, and a rearview mirror. UFO and Acerbis sell quick-mount front headlight plates. They also sell a combination rear fender extension, license plate mount, and a tail/brake light that can be bolted to the underside of the fender. The parts that connect the lighting coil to the lights include a wiring loom, handlebar switch, and voltage regulator, available from Moose Racing. If you want to make your bike DOT legal, you'll need a hydraulic brake light switch. Companies like Baja Designs and Dakar make all-inclusive kits with headlight, taillight, and license mounting bracket, horn, turn signals, brake switches, speedometer, and handlebar switch sets.

Electrex makes a complete ignition and lighting coil ring that is easily replaced by using a hand impact driver to remove the three number 2 Phillips screws.

PROJECT 18	Installing an SFB Racing Flywheel Weight

Time: 30 minutes

Tools: Ratchet and sockets 8, 14, and 17 mm, Allen sockets 4, 8, and 10 mm, 19-mm open-end wrench, ft-lbs torque wrench, electric or pneumatic impact wrench, Honda flywheel puller part number 07AMC-MEBA100, dead-shot plastic mallet

Talent: ★★

Tab: $125

Parts: Left-side cover gasket, SFB flywheel weight

Benefits: Less wheel spin on acceleration, better engine braking on deceleration

A flywheel weight reduces the moment of inertia of a crankshaft to prevent the engine from revving up too quickly on acceleration, and provides greater flywheel inertia for more effective engine braking when the throttle is closed. Contrary to popular belief, a flywheel weight doesn't improve low-end torque. That can only be accomplished with an increase in cylinder pressure. The SFB flywheel weight is available in sizes of 9, 11, and 16 ounces. Here is a step-by-step procedure on how to install an SFB flywheel weight:

1) Drain the crankcase oil from the left-side drain bolt, capture the oil in a sealed plastic container, and recycle it at an auto repair shop.

2) Remove the shift lever and the bolts that retain the left-side engine cover. Tap on the cover with a plastic mallet to break the gasket loose while pulling the cover off. The flywheel magnet also provides magnetic force that holds the cover down. Take care not to put your bare fingertips between the cover's gasket surface and the case, because if you slip, the magnetic force will pull the cover down and cut your fingers.

3) Pull the cover off, turn it to the side out of the way, wipe the remaining oil out of the cover, and clean the gasket surfaces of the cover and case.

4) Use the electric or pneumatic impact wrench to remove the flywheel nut and washer.

5) The Honda flywheel puller has a protective end cap that prevents damage to the oil jet on the end of the crankshaft during flywheel removal. The puller threads are left-hand, so turn the puller counter-clockwise until it bottoms out. Use a 19-mm open-end wrench to hold the puller base, and thread the center bolt clockwise until it is tight. Tap on the end of the puller bolt with a dead-shot plastic mallet— not a metal hammer! Tighten the center bolt a bit more and tap it again; repeat this procedure until the flywheel pops off the crankshaft. Take care not to lose the flywheel Woodruff key that aligns the flywheel precisely on the crankshaft.

6) The SFB flywheel weight is a two-piece assembly that fits in the back side and inside of the flywheel. There are two locating pins; rotate the weight so the two locating pins slide into the holes in the flywheel, and the four holes in the weight align with the holes in the flywheel. Set the flywheel front-side down on a bench, press the weight down into the flywheel, and use a plastic mallet to tap the weight evenly down flush to the flywheel.

7) Apply Blue Loctite to the four Allen mounting bolts. Use a 4-mm Allen socket and torque wrench to tighten the bolts to 6 ft-lbs in a diagonal pattern. Position the Woodruff key parallel to the centerline of the crankshaft, so the end that faces you appears a bit high. If the key is too low, the flywheel will not firmly seat on the taper and it could shake loose and damage the crankshaft and the generator.

8) Thread on the washer and nut and prepare to torque the flywheel nut to 64 ft-lbs. You have to hold the crankshaft from the right side in order to torque it properly. This involves removing the 10-mm Allen cap from the lower front of the right-side engine

cover in order to gain access to the 8-mm Allen bolt threaded to the end of the crankshaft. Use an 8-mm socket and ratchet to hold the crank bolt while you torque the flywheel nut. If you feel comfortable with an impact wrench you can just use that, since the flywheel nut is unlikely to unthread, considering the direction of rotation.

9) Now you can install a new gasket, check the two alignment pins, install the left-side cover, and tighten the bolts. Don't forget to add oil to the crankcase before starting the engine.

The SFB flywheel weight is a ring that mounts on the backside of the flywheel. Loctite is applied to the threads and the weight centers on a series of pins on the flywheel.

Clamp the flywheel with soft aluminum jaws and a vise to hold it while torquing the mounting bolts.

Chapter 9
LUBRICATION SYSTEM

Project 19

- Routine Cleaning
- Changing to a Stainless Steel Filter
- Installing a Baja Designs Oil Tank

Routine Cleaning

Even if you change the filter and the oil frequently, the sump screen will still accumulate metal particles. The CRF250 and 450 have different sump screens. The 250's setup is easy to clean; just remove the left-side engine cover, pull the screen out, and clean it. The screen is shaped like a flat panel, and it slides into a slot in the cases. The 450 has a pick-up tube and scoop that holds the filter screen. You must remove the flywheel in order to unbolt the pick-up tube. The yellow plastic gear is what drives the oil pump, which is located between the crankcases. While you've got the flywheel off, check the plastic gear for stripped teeth.

Changing to a Stainless-Steel Filter

A reusable filter is only as good as your cleaning practices. If you don't have a pressurized, filtered solvent tank, stick to disposable paper filters. If you are determined to convert to a stainless-steel, cleanable filter, here are tips on cleaning and priming the filter during servicing.

Cleaning Tip: Buy a parts washing tank with a pump and hose fitting. Companies like Harbor Freight sell setups like these, with 5 gallons of solvent, for only $120. You can insert the tank's hose end inside the filter so it forces the metal outward.

Priming Tip: Soak the filter in oil for 10 minutes before putting it in the engine.

Above Right: The CRF250 has a sump screen that slides out when the left-side engine cover is removed. You can clean it with solvent or brake cleaner.

Right: The CRF450 has a sump scoop that requires the flywheel to be removed in order to clean it. Both the 250 and 450 use a plastic gear to drive the oil pump from the balancer shaft. When debris circulates through the engine, the gear teeth wear and the pump stops working. Check the teeth for gash marks like this gear has.

PROJECT 19 | Installing a Baja Designs Oil Tank

Time: 1 hour

Tools: Ratchet and sockets 8, 10, 12, and 14 mm

Talent: ★★

Tab: $500

Parts: Baja Designs oil tank and bash plate

Benefits: Longer riding time interval between reoiling, lower oil temperatures due to increased volume

The advent of high-capacity, off-road fuel tanks made it necessary to expand and improve the lubrication system to match the new longer refueling intervals. Baja Designs makes an oil tank that increases the capacity of the lubrication system and provides a recirculation and collection passageway for the blowby gases. The system must be used with a matching bash plate that protects the oil tank under the front side of the engine.

1) Drain the crankcase oil and remove the drain plug, disconnect the crankcase vent hose from the valve cover and air boot.

2) Connect the oil line to the Baja oil tank and the drain plug bolt hole. Plug the air boot with the cap provided in the kit.

3) Mount the oil tank in the bash plate and the plate to the frame with the bolts and brackets provided.

4) Fill the crankcase slowly—it will take a little longer for the extra oil to seep into the oil tank—until the proper level shows in the sight glass.

SECTION 3
CHASSIS PROJECTS

Chapter 10
FRAME, PIVOTS, AND LINKAGE

Projects 20–21

- Magnafluxing the Frame for Damage Inspection
- Projects to Protect the Chassis
- Quick Grease Job
- Rebuilding the Swingarm and Linkage with a Pivot Works Kit

PROJECT 20	Magnafluxing the Frame for Damage Inspection

Time: 15 minutes

Tools: Flashlight and Magnaflux kit

Talent: ★

Tab: $20

Parts: Magnaflux Spot Check

Benefits: Peace of mind that the frame and swingarm do not have structural flaws that could cause a crash or expensive damage

The term Magnaflux was coined by a company of the same name, which invented a method and apparatus for identifying stress cracks in ferrous metals. The machine used a jig and ring to mount the part, and then an electromagnetic field was produced around the parts. A canister was used to sprinkle tiny metallic particles over the part, and the magnetic field enabled the particles to flow to cracks in the part's surface. This worked great for ferrous metals, but for nonferrous metals, like aluminum and magnesium, another process needed to be invented. A three-part spray product called Magnaflux Spot Check was produced to clean and identify a particular area where a stress crack may be suspected. For our CRF project, we'll look at the critical areas of a frame and swingarm where cracks are likely to occur. These areas include the neck, linkage stay-bar mounts, front and bottom engine mounts, foot-peg mounts, and the swingarm near the pivot axle

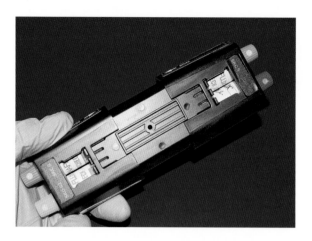

This kit is a Magnaflux Spot-Check special dye for locating cracks in aluminum parts.

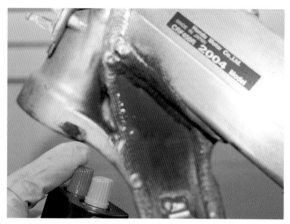

The dye flows into cracks, making them visible. In this picture, a frame neck is being examined.

and rear axle. The three-part Magnaflux kit includes a cleaner, dye penetrant, and developer.

1) Start by power washing the obvious dirt and oil from the frame so you don't waste too much of the cleaner. Spray the cleaner over the suspected area, towel dry, and spray the dye.
2) After a few minutes, spray some cleaner on a towel and wipe off the top layer of the dye. Now, spray the developer. As it dries, cracks will start to appear in dark red lines.

If there are any cracks in a frame, subframe, or swingarm, you'll need to strip down the affected part completely because it will have to be repaired with TIG welding. TIG stands for Tungsten Inert Gas and is the only welding method recommended for repairing aluminum. Look in a business phone book for welding shops that offer this welding process. Welding aluminum requires some preparation with a three-step process—grinding a V-shaped channel in the crack, preheating the area to 400 degrees Fahrenheit, then welding—in order to get the correct penetration. Take care not to leave the CDI (capacitive discharge ignition) or ignition coil attached to the frame, as the current used in TIG welding can damage them.

Quick Grease Job

Time: 15 minutes

Tools: Ratchet and sockets 14, 17, 19, and 22 mm, brass drift rod, hammer, grease gun

Talent: ★

Tab: $5

Parts: Moly-based or waterproof grease

Benefits: Reduces friction in the suspension system and prevents expensive damage to the linkage, swingarm, pivots, bearings, and rear shock

1) To grease the swingarm and linkage, start by removing these parts in this order: seat, subframe, brake pedal, top shock bolt, swingarm bolt, and both linkage bolt nuts.
2) Slide the linkage bolts back about halfway, then remove the end cap and inject grease into the needle bearing and bushings.
3) Clean and lube the spherical bearing of the top shock mount. Roll the bearing around in the shock mount and push grease or moly paste over the ball and cup.
4) Reinstall the bolts and torque the nuts to 58 ft-lbs. Torque the swingarm to 61 ft-lbs, and the top shock nut to 40 ft-lbs.

Projects to Protect the Chassis

CRFs have a lot of sensitive components that are easily damaged by rocks and debris common in off-road riding. Logs and rocks snag rear brake levers and bend discs. Aluminum frame tubes get crushed and scuffed on whoops, logs, and boulders. Radiators get tweaked from the side loads of crashes. Engine cases are vulnerable to hits from the front. Fortunately, there are a lot of aftermarket companies that make excellent products to protect your investment and save you from expensive damage.

Skid, Glide, and Bash Plates

Guards to protect the bottom of the frame and engine include skid plates that cover the engine cases and fit between the frame rails. Also available are glide plates that extend to the outer edges of the frame tubes, enabling the bike to glide across obstacles without being grabbed. Bash plates, the biggest guards, wrap up and around the frame tubes and crankcases. They are essential for riding over boulders, and if you buy an aftermarket oil tank, you will definitely need a bash plate to mount and protect the tank.

Brake Fins

A brake fin is a heavy-duty wedge of aluminum that fastens on the swingarm in front of the rear brake disc to protect it from bending on rocks and logs.

Radiator Crush Guards

There are two types of radiator guards: thin metal covers, and more durable guards with crush pro-tection. Crush protection means that the guards include long bars that extend from the outside of the radiators to the frame, so if you tip the bike on its sides, the radiators won't become crushed or tweaked out of alignment.

Frame Guards

Frame guards fasten to the junction between the subframe's lower mounts and the frame. They are intended as smooth covers to prevent your boots from snagging on the frame while riding. They also serve to protect the sides of the frame when the bike slides along the ground in a crash.

Engine Guards

Engine case guards are made of thick aluminum. They replace the stock plastic shields mounted to the front of the frame in front of the engine's side covers.

Brake Pedal Cables

Brake pedal cables consist of a thick, stainless steel wire with a loop on one end and a mounting tab on the other. They are designed to prevent thin branches from wedging between the rear brake pedal and the frame, which can tear off the pedal. The cables can also help when riding through deep ruts. Considering that brake pedals cost nearly $100, a cheap brake pedal cable is a good investment.

For more information on products to protect the frame, check out product reviews in *Dirt Rider* magazine or look online at www.dirtrider.com.

PROJECT 21	Rebuilding the Swingarm and Linkage with a Pivot Works Kit

Time: 2 hours

Tools: Ratchet and sockets 14, 17, 19, and 22 mm, brass drift rod, hammer, grease gun, Race Tech bushing press kit

Talent: ★★

Tab: $80–$190

Parts: Pivot Works swingarm, linkage, and shock-bearing kits; Sunnen press lube, moly grease

Benefits: Reduces friction in the suspension system and prevents expensive damage to the linkage, swingarm, pivots, bearings, and rear shock

Although the parts of a Pivot Works kit are virtually identical to original Honda parts, the main advantage to these kits is that all the parts are packaged together to reduce the cost and hassle of looking up all the part numbers and assembling the parts in order. If you keep the original parts greased, following the procedure outlined in Quick Grease Job (page 83), they will last indefinitely. However, if the seals fail and the bearings get contaminated with water or dirt, they will corrode and be extremely difficult to remove with the methods listed in the Honda service manual.

Installing the new parts is easy; removing the old parts is hit or miss. Depending on usage and service life, the old parts could drive out easily, or be stubborn and push your anger management level into orbit. It's easy to damage an expensive swingarm when you're angry and not sure what to do, so be patient and think things through. Following are two procedures to remove old bearings and bushings based on the level of corrosion.

Procedure for Lubed Parts
1) Pry out the old caps and seals.
2) Use a punch to drive out the bushings in either direction.
3) Scrape out the old bearing needles with a knife and a magnet.
4) Match a large socket to the outer edge of the race (that's the steel sleeve pressed into the swingarm).

The socket will work as a driver, or you can use a seal-driver kit available from an auto parts stores.
5) Carefully support the swingarm to prevent bending during this next procedure. It is best to use a press to remove races, but if the races are still lubed

Moly grease won't melt away like other greases.

85

they may be driven out with the socket or driver and a dead-shot plastic mallet.

6) Apply heat from a propane torch or electric heat gun for a few minutes in an attempt to expand the swingarm away from the race.

7) Press or hammer out the race. If the races came out easily, take a swatch of fine sandpaper and polish the race cavity in the swingarm.

Procedure for Rusted Bearings

If the bearings and bushings ran without lube for too long and are rusted, don't try to press or drive them out. Try this procedure, which you won't read in any factory service manual, because the factories never work on old bikes, but we have to! When the race is corroded it's impossible to press out, so it has to be slit down its length in order to release the pressure holding the race into the swingarm or linkage.

Use a die grinder to slice the race of the bearing so it collapses, making it easy to remove.

When the swingarm bolt is hopelessly stuck, like on this KTM200, you have two choices: press or saw. Here the bike is disassembled and mounted in a 55-ton hydraulic press.

Tools

You'll need a die grinder with a stone- or carbide-pointed bit to grind through the hardened race. For this example, we demonstrate using a Dremel Moto-Tool. Miscellaneous tools include a drift punch and dead-shot mallet, pliers, and sanding rolls.

1) Use the Moto-Tool to grind a channel down the length of the race. Take care not to grind too deep, just enough to cut through the race.
2) Once the race is cut, you can either knock it out with a drift punch or grab it with pliers to extract it.
3) The cavity in the swingarm or linkage must be cleaned of corrosion debris and polished before you attempt to install the new races.

How to Install the New Parts

Once you have removed the old parts and cleaned and polished the race cavity, you can install the new parts. The races and bearings are loaded, greased, and have a plastic sleeve inserted to hold them together during installation.

1) Coat the races with Sunnen press lube and install them into the swingarm to a depth that just allows for the fit of the seal and dust cap.
2) Slide the bushings in and the plastic sleeves out. Put a dab of grease around the bushing ends for the seals to have something to pack up against.

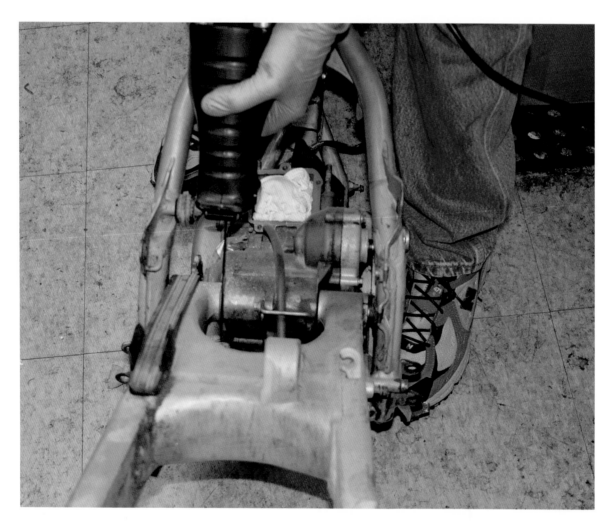

The last resort for removing rusted swingarm and linkage pivot bolts is using a reciprocating hacksaw. In this picture, the stubborn KTM200 is having its swingarm pivot bolt sliced into three pieces to separate the swingarm from the frame.

Chapter 11
STEERING AND CONTROLS
Projects 22–25

- How to Lube and Tension the Steering Head
- Installing a Pivot Works Steering Head Kit
- Upgrading with an Aftermarket Triple Clamp Kit
- Installing a Fat Handlebar Kit
- How to Install a Steering Damper
- Custom Ergonomic Projects

The steering head of a motorcycle is the most neglected component of a dirt bike, because it keeps working until the point of failure. Steering head bearings require a high-temperature grease and periodic tensioning. New product trends have favored innovative designs in controls like tapered-wall handlebars that absorb vibration, pivoting levers that resist breaking, and throttle cams to tame big-bore four-strokes. This chapter will show you how to make your bike easier to control.

How to Lube and Tension the Steering Head

1) To grease and torque the steering head, start by removing the handlebars to gain access to the stem nut.
2) Remove the stem nut and loosen the top clamp bolts so the top clamp can be removed. Loosen the spanner nut with a hammer and punch.
3) Unthread the spanner nut and drop the steering stem a few inches to gain access to the bearing. Visually check the condition of the bearings. If they are rusty or the roller cage is cracked, the bearings and races need to be replaced.
4) Apply grease to the top and bottom bearings, then reinstall the bottom clamp, spanner nut, top clamp, and hex nut. The steering head tension will need to be adjusted a few times as the bike breaks in.
5) Start by pushing up the steering stem into the frame. Hand-tighten the spanner nut and use the punch and hammer to tighten it about 1/3 turn. Install the top clamp and torque the nut to 105 ft-lbs. Now check the steering tension. With the bike on a stand, there should be a small bit of resistance to turn the bars in each direction.

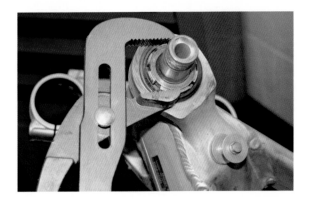

Tension the spanner nut by hand. If you overtighten this nut, the bearings will break. Setting the torque on the steering head is by trial and error. Snug the spanner, tighten down the top clamp nut to 50 ft-lbs, and test how much force it takes to turn the handlebars. It's best to have a little drag on the steering, that way you'll know that the tension on the steering head is right.

PROJECT 22	Installing a Pivot Works Steering Head Kit

Time: 2 hours

Tools: Ratchet and sockets 10, 12, 32 mm, foot-pounds torque wrench, hammer, drift rod, 20-ton hydraulic press, propane torch or heat gun, press tools like spacers and slugs, press lube, grease

Talent: ★ ★ ★ ★ ★

Tab: $50

Parts: Pivot Works Steering Head Rebuild Kit

Benefit: Smoother steering, less headshake, better turning

Pivot Works specializes in all-inclusive bearing, bushing, race, and seal kits for late-model Japanese dirt bikes. The procedure for removing the bearing from the steering stem and the races in the frame requires the use of a 20-ton hydraulic press and a race-installing kit. If you doubt your abilities, take your bike to a Honda dealer.

Here is the procedure: drop the forks from the bottom clamp, remove the handlebars, hex nut, top clamp, spanner nut, and bottom clamp. Discard the top bearing, and wipe the races clean of grease. Use a propane torch to heat the bottom outside of the frame neck for five minutes. Insert a long punch through the opposite end of the neck and rest the tip of the punch on the inner diameter of the race. Carefully strike the punch at four equidistant points (such as north, south, east, and west) until the race drops out of the neck.

1) To install the new bearing races, start by placing the new races in the freezer for two hours.

2) Use a swatch of medium-grit sandpaper to polish the neck's race cavities to remove any rough spots left over from removing the old races.

3) Heat each of the neck's race cavities with a propane torch for three minutes. This is very important, because the race to neck is an interference fit. The race is a larger diameter than the cavity in the neck. Expanding the race cavity and contracting the race will make it easier to install using a seal and bearing driver with a dead-shot mallet.

Changing the Lower Steering Stem Bearing

This is a difficult procedure that requires a 20-ton press and a variety of fixtures for supporting and pressing the stem. If you are installing an aftermarket triple clamp, you may also need to use this same procedure to swap the stem to the new bottom clamp.

1) Prepare for pressing by heating the bottom clamp from the underside with a propane torch for three minutes. This will serve to expand the clamp and break the bond of the locking agent

This top steering stem bearing is rusted because it wasn't greased often.

89

that is applied at the factory. Take care to support the bottom clamp in the press, using a set of V-blocks positioned closely to the stem. If the support is spaced too wide, then the clamp could break and pinch the stem.

2) Thread the large nut flush to the top of the stem to press on the nut, rather than directly on the soft aluminum threads of the stem. If you damage the stem, you'll have to buy a whole new bottom clamp, because they aren't sold separately. Carefully press the stem out through the bottom of the clamp and remove the bottom bearing. For information on installing a new bottom bearing, skip to step four of the procedure for installing an aftermarket triple clamp.

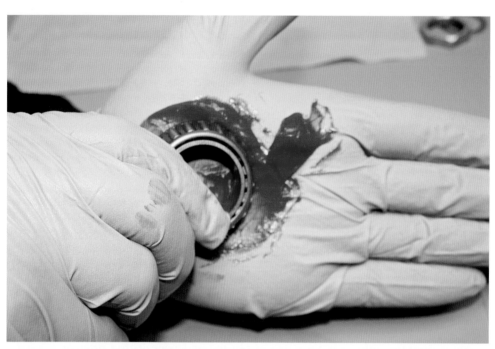

Grease a tapered roller bearing by wiping it through a dab of grease on your hand.

The Pivot Works kit comes with everything you need to do the whole job.

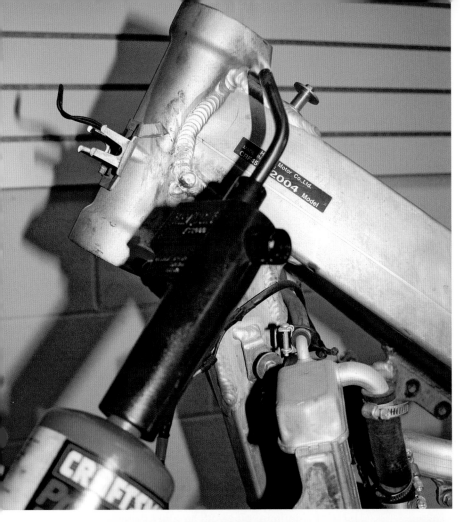

If you have to replace the bearing races in the neck, heat the aluminum around the bear for five minutes before you try to drive out the races.

Motion Pro makes a handy installation tool for tapered races. It uses slugs the same size, and the bearing can be tightened on a threaded shaft so they seat evenly in the frame. You can also use a large-diameter socket or aluminum slug and a hammer.

PROJECT 23 | Upgrading with an Aftermarket Triple Clamp Kit

Time: 30 minutes

Tools: Hydraulic press and spacing parts

Talent: ★★★★★

Tab: $250–$500

Parts: Aftermarket triple clamp kit

Benefits: Quicker steering

If you are installing an aftermarket triple clamp, use this procedure for installing the new triple.

1) Use a swatch of medium-grit sandpaper to polish down the old locking agent and galling marks from the stem and bottom clamp.

2) Place the stem in the freezer for two hours. Heat the bottom clamp in the oven to 175 degrees Fahrenheit for 30 minutes. When the parts are ready for installation, apply a dab of Green Loctite to the stem area that interfaces with the clamp.

3) Support the clamp close to the stem hole and press the stem in from the underside of the clamp until it bottoms out.

4) To install the lower bearing, prepare the bearing by forcing wheel-bearing grease through the rollers. Install the bottom seal washer and slide the bearing down onto the stem until it binds. Set the bottom clamp on a solid plate so the stem won't press back out when you press on the bearing. Use a piece of aluminum pipe with an inner diameter slightly larger than the stem's outer diameter, and an overall length greater than that of the stem.

5) Press the bearing down until it bottoms out on the clamp.

Follow the procedure on page 88 for tensioning the steering head.

Heat the bottom clamp and bearing for a few minutes before pressing out the stem.

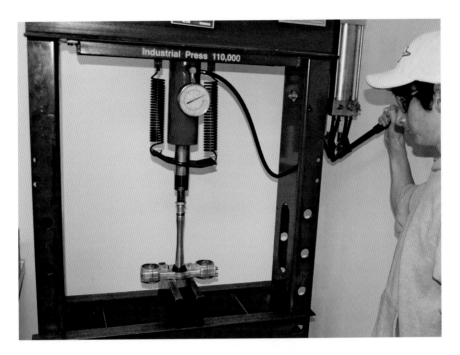

Support the bottom of the clamp so it doesn't bend. Leave the nut threaded flush on top for the most surface area to press on. Stand to the side of the press and wear safety glasses in case something breaks loose.

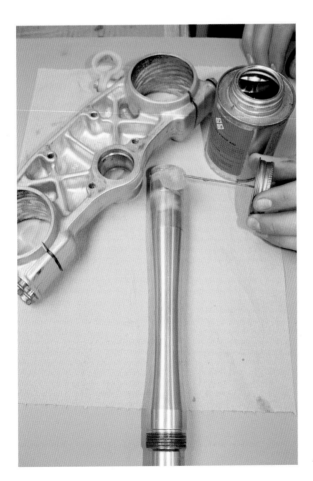

A dab of assembly oil or anti-seize will prevent gauling when the stem is pressed into the clamp.

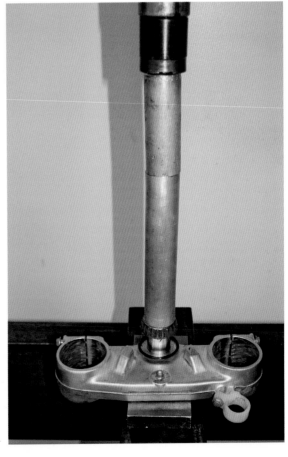

Press the bearing on with a long aluminum tube that closely matches the diameter of the inner bearing race.

Installing a Fat Handlebar Kit

Time: 15 minutes

Tools: Ratchet and sockets 8, 10, 12 mm

Talent: ★

Tab: $100–$220

Parts: Handlebar and clamp kit

Benefits: More bar flex, less vibration, less forearm pump

Tapered-wall handlebars were first invented by Answer Products under the brand name Pro-Taper. Now other manufacturers like Moose Racing, Renthal, and Magura make similar products. The advantage of these handlebars is that they flex a bit on hard impacts, rather than transferring the force into the rider's hands and wrists. Tapered-wall handlebars require special mounting brackets. The handlebar diameter is larger than the original handlebars at the mounting point.

Fitting Performance Controls
Performance controls include Moose Racing aluminum throttle tubes, G2 throttle-cam systems, ASV unbreakable lever sets, and Works Connection pivoting perches with ball-bearing pivots and quick adjusters. It's all a matter of personal preference, and generally speaking, these aftermarket controls are designed to save you money from crash damage. The G2 throttle cam systems include three different cam-profile cable holders and an aluminum throttle tube. The cams range from quick turn to slow turn. The quick-turn cam is ideal for motocross racers on CRF250s. The slow-turn cam is great for beginner motocross or tight-woods riders looking for smoother throttle control or less radical response when exiting turns.

PROJECT 24	How to Install a Steering Damper

Time: 20 minutes

Tools: Ratchet and sockets 8, 10, 32 mm, plastic mallet, Allen wrench set, foot-pounds torque wrench

Talent: ★

Tab: $450

Parts: Ohlins GPR or Scott's brand steering damper

Benefits: No head shaking, more precise turning and straight-line stability, less forearm pump

Steering dampers help the front wheel self-steer by damping the oscillations that can be transferred from the tire into the handlebars. Steering dampers are especially useful to off-road riders who operate dirt bikes at speeds beyond their intended design limit.

Ohlins is a Swedish manufacturer of fluid damping and drive components like telescopic forks, rotary and conventional shocks, front-wheel-drive systems, and steering dampers. The Ohlins GPR steering damper is a universal component that has model-specific mounting parts, and which features a dial to adjust the damping force while riding. The main unit bolts to the handlebar clamps, and the stationary mount is clamped to the top of the frame's neck. Following is the step-by-step procedure for installing a GPR steering damper.

1) Remove the handlebar clamp bolts and loosen the four 10-mm bolts on the top clamp.
2) Loosen and remove the 32-mm nut that retains the top clamp to the steering stem.
3) Slide the stationary collar down onto the frame neck, align the opening in the six o'clock position, and tighten the Allen pinch bolts.

This bike has a set of Applied triple clamps, Pro Taper handlebars, and a Scott's (Ohlins) steering damper.

4) Reinstall the top clamp, torque the 32-mm nut to 50 ft-lbs, and tighten the four top-clamp bolts to 12 ft-lbs.

5) Install the handlebars and clamps, fit the GPR damper to the two rear clamp bolts, set the handlebar position to your personal preference, and torque the bolts to 12 ft-lbs.

A steering damper has a mounting ring that clamps around the top race holders of the frame's neck. The rotary damper mounts to the handlebar lamp. An adjuster enables riders to change the damping force on the fly.

PROJECT 25 | Custom Ergonomic Projects

Time: 20 minutes and up

Tools: Varies by project

Talent: ★★ to ★★★★★

Tab: $0 to $500

Parts: Springs, shocks, forks, shock linkage, and custom-fabricated bits

Benefits: A bike that fits the rider like a glove

Custom Ergonomic Projects

CRFs are only available in one size, but riders come is all shapes and sizes. Matching your unique dimensions to your motorcycle is critical to comfort and control. Dimensional factors like the distance from the seat to foot pegs, ground, and handlebars, the width of the bars, and the relationship of the foot pegs to the shifter and brake lever, are all part of the ergonomics equation. Ergonomics for dirt bikes means how comfortable and controllable the bike is to ride. Dirt bike magazines rate the ergonomics of bikes in tests, but only for the particular profile of that rider. If you are not a 5-foot 9-inch, 155-pound, 24-year-old male, then we have some projects that you should consider for customizing the ergonomics of your bike to suit your height, weight, age, and reach.

Projects for Big Guys

Big guys like to increase the distance between the seat and pegs, the seat and the bars, and the shift lever to the foot peg. There are some aftermarket products that help accomplish these tasks. Fastway makes Evolution 2 series foot pegs for $110 that feature a pin kit that enables you to move the foot pegs down and back, which is great for accommodating boot sizes over 10 inches. The pegs are also wider, and have adjustable screws to bias the front-to-back height. Answer Products makes Pro-Taper handlebars with risers and forward-mounted clamps. Most tall riders choose the Doug Henry bend, which is the tallest Pro-Taper handlebar. Pro-Taper bars start in cost at $130, plus the clamps, which are model-specific. Gutz Racing

specializes in taller, stiffer seat foam and covers to match your bike. Gutz can add as much as 4 inches to the center of the seat and make the seat level from the fender to the tank.

Suspension components can be ergonomically altered to suit guys who are either heavy, tall, or both. Jeremy Wilkey of MX-Tech says, "Taller riders greatly change the combined center of gravity of the bike and rider because of the obvious leverage that they exert on the bike. Tall guys feel more comfortable standing up, so the suspension components must be valved and sprung to suit. The rear shock needs a stiffer-than-average spring, because the rider is effectively shifting the combined center of gravity toward the back of the bike."

Projects for Not-So-Big Guys

Vertically challenged riders have the most trouble adapting to modern dirt bikes because they have difficulty touching the ground. The same type of components can be altered to suit riders with shorter-than-average dimensions. Low-rise bars, raised and forward-mounted foot pegs, and cut-down seat foam make a difference, but the single biggest change that can be made to a bike is limiting the travel of the suspension components. Shorter bikes are generally considered dysfunctional in the suspension department, but if the modifications are done correctly, the only thing a short bike gives up is ground clearance (which only requires that a rider be careful riding ruts). Considering the fact that 12 inches of suspension travel has 4 inches of spring sag, you might wonder what a bike with 8 inches of travel handles like. How's this: a travel-limited CRF has a lower center of gravity, which makes the bike more comfortable to turn in the tight woods or on stadium tracks. When Ricky Carmichael raced for Honda, he had his suspension tuner travel-limit his supercross bikes 2 inches and had the seat foam cut down another 2 inches. So obviously there is no shame in lowering a bike if the G.O.A.T. can win championships on a travel-limited bike.

Limiting Suspension Travel

The ride height of a dirt bike can be reduced in three ways: cutting down the seat foam, shortening the subframe tubes, or limiting the suspension travel. Riders who choose to limit the travel of the forks and shock may do it to make the bike more comfortable for their height or to change the bike's geometry for better handling. Limiting the suspension travel lowers the bike's center of gravity, making it easier to turn for racing in places like tight woods, flat track, and supermoto.

Jeremy Wilkey of MX-Tech has some general rules for travel-limiting bikes for different applications and rider types. For motocross and off-road, the maximum travel-limiting for forks and shocks should be no more than 2 inches, otherwise the compromises in suspension performance outweigh the benefits of lowering the bike. Jeremy tends to soften the low-speed compression damping of the rear shock to counteract the change in the starting point of the motion ratio of the shock linkage. For sports like dirt track, the bike's geometry must be radically changed, biasing the weight to the front end by limiting the fork travel 4 to 5 inches and the rear shock by 3 to 4 inches. This serves to lower the bike's center of gravity and move it forward in order to maintain a swingarm angle 3 to 4 degrees for maximum traction. Jeremy says, "The biggest problem with limiting the rear shock travel is that you have less space/time to dissipate the energy of a bump."

Limiting travel can be as simple as installing spacers on the shock shaft or the forks' piston rod during normal maintenance. The spacers are available in 12.5- and 25-mm increments, and sell for $30 each. Determining how much to limit the travel of the front versus the rear suspension is based on your riding demands and the length of your legs. Consult a professional suspension tuner to configure the best setup for you.

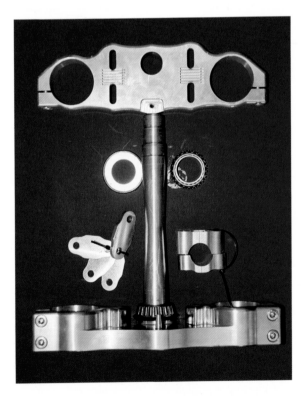

These triple clamps have adjustable-position clamp mounts and different thickness clamps so big guys can raise the bars and mount them farther forward.

Rich Rohrich needed to lower the center of gravity on his CRF450 for dirt track and supermoto. The travel of the forks and shock is limited to 8 inches front and rear. The valving and spring rates were calculated and installed by MX-Tech.

Chapter 12
SUSPENSION PROJECTS

- Cartridge Fork Terminology
- Comprehensive Twin-Chamber Servicing
- Installing Enzo Subtanks
- Installing MX-Tech Mid and Base Valve Kits

The Twin-Chamber Showa cartridge forks used on all CRF models are sturdy and well built. Seals and wipers wear quickly and require changing about twice per riding season. Seal-Savers help stretch the service time but they must be cleaned every ride for best results. Some riders prefer to customize their forks with heavier springs, subtanks, mid valves or base valves, or by limiting travel. This chapter is a guide to step-by-step servicing and tips on installing aftermarket accessories.

Tools of the Trade

In order to service the Showa forks, you'll need some special tools as well as some common sockets and wrenches. Starting from the top of the fork, an eight-point, 50-mm box wrench and split-collar seal and bushing driver will be needed for routine servicing, as well as a seal-bullet to protect the seal from tearing upon installation on the fork tube. To remove the cartridge from the fork tubes, a straight, flat wrench is required. A six-point, 21-mm socket and ratchet fits the rebound adjuster bolt.

Cartridge Fork Myths and Truths

Myth—Midstroke harshness is caused by excessive mid valve compression damping.

Truth—Midstroke harshness is caused by excessive progressive elements (air spring and wire spring load) compounding each other against softer compression damping rates.

Myth—Changing the ICS results in an improvement of compression-damping characteristics.

Truth—Changing the ICS only affects the overall spring rate.

Myth—Switching the weight of the oil changes the damping.

Truth—Oil weight changes affect only the lower end of the damping spectrum.

Myth—Midstroke harshness can be improved by reducing the mid valve compression or changing the spring rates of the ICS and main spring.

Truth—Midstroke harshness can be improved by increasing the active compression damping and reducing the air spring force with a lower oil height.

A set of shaft blocks will be needed to clamp the round tubes of the forks. Race Tech makes inexpensive universal aluminum shaft blocks that will ensure the sensitive tubes don't get damaged when clamped in a vise.

Some other assorted tools will be needed, like small, straight-blade screwdrivers, a 6-inch vise, pointed scribe, light-duty locking agent, spool of Teflon tape, and tube of seal grease.

Cleaning the parts and capturing the waste oil are important considerations. Most automotive garages and express oil stations accept small sealed containers of waste oil. The parts are best cleaned with a high-flashpoint mineral spirits solvent like PB Parts Blaster, available from auto parts stores like Pep Boys. Mail-order companies such as Harbor Freight sell covered parts washers with a pump and brush, plus a 5-gallon container of solvent, for about $150 delivered.

Cartridge Fork Terminology

Active and Passive Valving: There are two valve assemblies in the fork leg. The compression valve assembly is the passive valve, because it is stationary and depends on the oil column to flow through it. The mid valve on the end of the cylinder rod is the active valve, because it travels through the oil column when the forks compress or rebound.

Air Spring: The air spring is a compression-resistance force that works mostly when the forks are nearly bottomed in travel. The air spring pressure is based on the volume of air versus the volume of oil in the fork leg, at the top and bottom of the travel range. The air-spring ratio is affected by the oil height. The higher the oil height, the greater the air-spring compression ratio.

Axle Clamp: The axle clamp is threaded and pinned to the inner fork tube.

Bushings and Seals: The bushings are the load-bearing surfaces of the fork tubes and cartridge cylinder. The seal and wiper are the hydraulic-sealing components of the fork leg.

Cartridge Cylinder: The main cylinder of the cartridge assembly holds the cylinder rod, mid valve, check valve spring, rebound valve, and rebound adjuster rod. The cylinder is topped with the compression adjuster assembly.

Check Valve Spring: The spring seated between the bottom of the cartridge cylinder and the piston of the cylinder rod.

Compression Valve Assembly: The cartridge connected to the fork cap. It contains the internal compression spring (ICS), piston, ring, and valves. The compression valve is the passive valve.

Cylinder Rod: The cylinder rod is the main shaft of the cartridge assembly. It holds the piston, ring, valves (mid and rebound), and rebound adjuster rod.

Fork Slider: The outer aluminum tube connected to the triple clamps.

Fork Tube: The inner steel tube connected to the axle clamp.

Hydraulic Stops and Cones: A tapered cone on the bottom of the cartridge cylinder that interfaces with another cone mounted in the bottom of the fork tube near the axle clamp. A hydraulic stop forms when the two cones bottom out, squeezing the oil.

ICS: The internal compression spring is part of the compression valve assembly. It seats between the piston and the end cap.

Main Spring: The long coil spring that fits inside the fork leg.

Mid Valve: The mid valve is a series of shims mounted to the top side of the piston on the cylinder rod. The mid valve is the active compression valve.

Rebound Adjuster Bolt: The rebound adjuster bolt is fastened to the bottom of the axle clamp. This bolt holds the forks together, clamping the cartridge to the outer tubes and the triple and axle clamps.

Rebound Adjuster Rod: The small-diameter tube that connects the clicker to the flow-control tapered needle in the piston.

Transfer Control Valve: The transfer control valve (TCV) is a large, plastic tube located inside the inner fork tube near the axle clamp. The TCV is a viscous damping system with a check valve and hydraulic bottoming cone providing resistance to the oil column.

PROJECT 26 | Comprehensive Twin-Chamber Servicing

Time: 2–3 hours

Tools: Race Tech cartridge fork tool set

Talent: ★★★

Tab: $95

Parts: Pivot Works Rebuild Kit, fork oil, grease

Benefits: Better handling

Maintenance Intervals

Modern two-staged sealed cartridge forks don't require as much maintenance as the older-style cartridge forks, because the cartridge is sealed from contamination produced from the fork tubes and springs. Here is a list of the typical tasks and intervals associated with servicing modern forks:

Seals and Wipers

High-performance seals with relatively low drag need to be changed about twice a season, or approximately every 40 hours. You can buy durable seals that require less maintenance, but the stiction will be so great that it will affect the damping performance.

Race Tech makes a variety of suspension tools; this is what you need to service Showa twin chamber forks.

Bushings

The bushings are the load-bearing surfaces of the fork. There are three bushings in each fork leg. The bushings are located in the slider tube, on the fork tube, and inside the fork cylinder. The bushings are very durable and don't wear quickly unless they become damaged during a seal and wiper change.

Outer Tube Oil Change

The outer fork tubes contain the oil that lubricates the seals and bushings and provide a means of tuning the air spring. There is no need to use high-quality expensive oil, just one with good lubrication properties. The service interval for cleaning and oil changing is the same as the seals and wipers, twice a season or every 40 hours, whichever is greater.

Cartridge Service

The cartridge needs to be cleaned about once per season or every 80–100 hours of usage. High-quality oil like Motorex 2.5 should be used, because its formulization best matches the cartridge bushings and bleed setups.

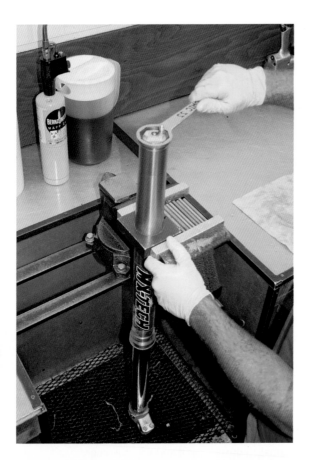

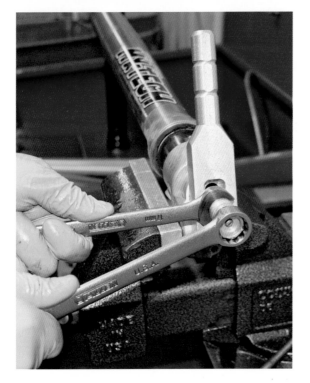

Top Left: Disassembling the Forks
Use a Race Tech eight-point, 50-mm box wrench to remove the outer fork cap. Depress the slider tube and drain the oil from the outer chamber. Capture the oil and recycle it at an automotive garage or oil express.

Bottom Left: Unthread the rebound adjuster bolt with a 21-mm socket while holding the axle clamp in a vise. The rebound adjuster bolt will separate from the fork tube, but it still needs to be unthreaded from the cylinder rod. Extend the cylinder rod by pushing on the top of the cartridge to expose the damper rod jam nut. Place a Race Tech flat wrench on the cylinder rod and loosen the jam nut and rebound adjuster bolt.

Above: Remove the cartridge assembly and the spring from the top of the fork leg. Clamp the upper part of the cylinder in a shaft block and vise, then use a box wrench to remove the compression-valve assembly. Pull to separate the compression valve from the cartridge cylinder.

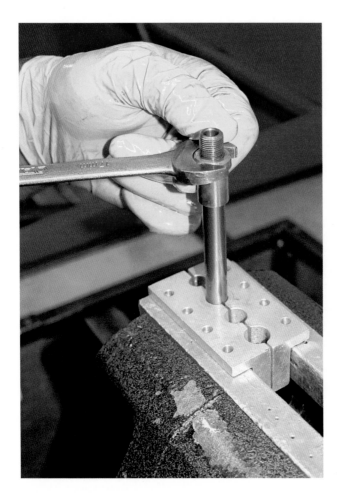

Disassemble the cartridge for cleaning. Start by clamping the cylinder rod in a shaft block and unthreading the jam nut. Now slide the cylinder rod out of the top of the cylinder. The best method for cleaning the oily components of the fork is a high-flash-point (120 degrees Fahrenheit) mineral-spirits solvent. Solvent breaks up the mixture of grease, oil, and metal debris that contaminates the forks. Commercially available products include PB Blaster, available from most auto parts stores. Non-chlorinated brake cleaner is the best choice for final cleaning. Allow the parts to drip dry.

Changing Seals, Wipers, and Bushings

The fork tube and slider must be separated to change the seals and bushings. Use a small, straight-blade screwdriver to pry off the wiper; now remove the circlip and slide the parts down the tube. Heat the lower part of the fork slider with a propane torch to expand the fork slider away from the outer bushing; this will make it easier to separate the tube and fork slider. This will also prevent the outer bushing from being pushed over the inner bushing, which can scrub off the Teflon coating.

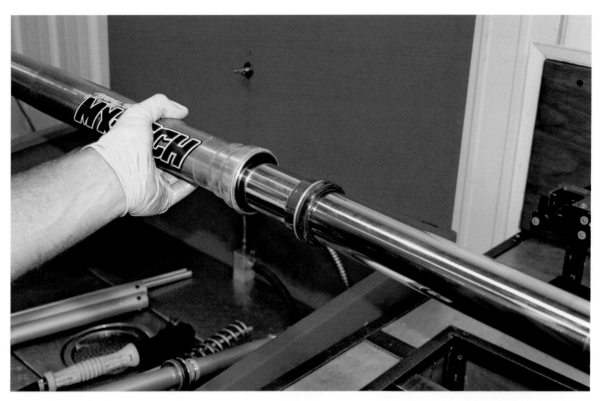

Grasp the fork tubes with your hands and quickly extend them several times until the tubes separate. The bushings, seals, circlip, and wiper will be retained on the inner fork tube. Now remove the fork tube bushing by spreading it with a screwdriver, and slide it off the end of the tube. Discard the old oil and dust seals and inspect the bushings for wear.

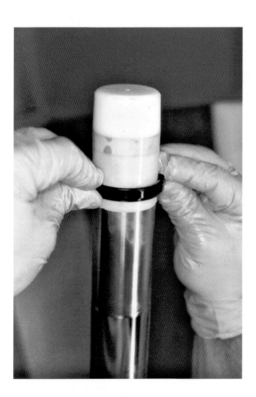

Put a dab of grease under the lip of the oil seal and dust wiper. Install a new wiper and bushing on the fork tube. Place a seal bullet or a plastic bag over the end of the fork tube to prevent damage to the new seal. Make sure to install seals, bushings, aluminum spacer, and circlip in the exact order.

Use a seal driver on the aluminum spacer to seat the outer bushing in the fork slider, and then use the driver on the seal. Install the circlip and use a plastic mallet to tap the wiper evenly into the slider. Set the fork tubes aside and get ready to assemble the inner cartridge.

Assembling the Cartridge

Wrap a piece of Teflon tape around the threads of the piston rod before inserting into the cylinder. This will prevent chafing of the internal seal, which is extremely difficult to replace. Insert the piston rod assembly into the cylinder using a 10-mm T-handle to manipulate the piston rod into place.

When installing the jam nut on the end of the piston rod, ensure that the jam nut is threaded all the way up on the piston rod. Clamp the cylinder in the shaft-block and tighten the vise so you can hold the cartridge upright for oil filling.

Overfill the cartridge to an oil height of about 100-mm from the top edge of the cylinder with Motorex 2.5 oil. You'll need a total of two bottles to refurbish both fork tubes. Perform nonpressurized bleeding of the cartridge by moving the rod a total of 1 inch up and down to help displace trapped air to the top of the cylinder. Stroke the rod about 30 times to bleed the cartridge, then wait 10 minutes for the air to bubble upward. Wipe a dab of grease on the O-ring prior to inserting it into the top of the cartridge. Tighten the fork cap hand-tight. Now perform pressurized bleeding, stroking the cartridge 2 inches or less for a total of 30 times. This will compress the remaining air bubbles and position them near the top for final bleeding. Clamp the bottom of the cartridge in the vise vertically. Compress the cartridge slowly through its full travel. Tip the cartridge to the side to drain the excess oil.

Insert the cartridge into the tube and compress the cartridge until the rod extends far enough to use the flat wrench. Install the long aluminum rebound-adjuster rod into the piston rod flush to the end, then slide the rebound-adjuster tab until it interlocks with the rebound rod. Tighten the rebound-adjuster bolt until it bottoms out on the rod, not the jam nut. There is the danger that the forks will be unequal lengths if you get this procedure wrong.

Filling the Outer Forks with Oil

The next step is to fill the outer fork tubes with 350cc of oil. The oil volume and height generates the air spring's progression. The lower the oil volume, the less progressive the effects of the air spring. The higher the volume, the more progressive your air spring will be. Consult your owner's manual for suggestions on oil volume for your riding demands. There are no bleeding considerations for the outer fork tubes. Tighten the fork cap hand-tight, because the triple clamp provides the extra torque to prevent the cap from unthreading.

Tighten the jam nut against the rebound adjuster by holding a wrench on the jam nut and a socket on the bolt. Take care when removing the flat wrench, because the spring pressure will cause the rebound adjuster to slam into place. Put a dab of grease on the threads of the rebound adjuster and tighten it into the fork tube to 25 ft-lbs.

PROJECT 27 | Installing Enzo Subtanks

Time: 1 hour

Tools: Drill, metric drill bits, tap handle, 8x1.0-mm tap, 9-mm reamer, depth caliper, 10-mm wrench, shaft blocks, Blue Loctite

Talent: ★★★★★

Tab: $350

Parts: Enzo carbon fiber subtanks, tap oil

Benefits: Plusher feel to the front forks and better bottoming resistance

Subtanks serve as a buffer to the air springs, allowing for the use of higher oil heights to increase bottoming resistance and reducing the effects of the high oil height when a rider hits braking bumps. They give a plusher feeling over braking bumps and reduce the shock on a rider's forearms on hard jump landings.

To install subtanks, the fork caps must be drilled, tapped, and reamed to accept the hose fitting.
1) Disassemble the base valve down to the fork cap using shaft blocks, a vise, and a 10-mm wrench. If you haven't ground the end of the base valve shaft already to install an aftermarket base valve, you'll need to do that before attempting to remove the nut (see below).
2) Remove the air bleeder screw and drill a 7-mm hole straight through the bleeder screw hole in the cap.
3) Tap the hole with an 8x1.0-mm tap; apply some oil to the tap to make it easier.
4) Now the hole must be reamed to accept an O-ring. Use a 9-mm reamer in the threaded hole to a depth of 2.5 mm.
5) Apply a dab of Blue Loctite to the hose fitting and thread it into the hole hand-tight.
Installing subtanks is a side project that can be done separately or together with servicing.

The Enzo subtanks are mounted to the fork sliders with a carbon fiber half-clamp. The hoses connect to the fork cap, and the tuning screw in the manifold is easily adjusted with a screwdriver.

The tank hoses connect through the old bleeder screw holes. The holes must be drilled, reamed, and tapped to accept the hose tank fittings.

The hose fittings are fastened to the fork caps.

PROJECT 28 | Installing MX-Tech Mid and Base Valve Kits

Time: 15 minutes extra during fork servicing

Tools: Grinding wheel, suspension tools

Talent: ★ ★ ★ ★

Tab: $250

Parts: MX-Tech mid and base valve kits, parts common to fork servicing

Benefits: Better handling due to improved front suspension action

There are a lot of theories reported in magazines regarding the midspeed performance of cartridge forks and the feeling of harshness. Midstroke harshness is caused by excessive progressive elements (air spring and wire spring load) compounding each other against softer compression damping rates.

The MX-Tech mid valve kit is the first aftermarket kit of its kind and it's designed to increase the lower and mid-speed compression damping while reducing the stock mid valve's tendency to either produce insufficient or excessive compression damping. Typical rider benefits include increased bottoming resistance without a corresponding increase in harshness.

The MX-Tech kit offers some measure of customization based on stock and aftermarket base valves, spring rates, rider skill level, and terrain type. A tuning chart and supply of shims are also supplied so a tuner can revalve to suit a rider's individual needs.

The mid valve is located on the end of the piston rod and retained by a 10-mm nut. The end of the shaft is peened so that has to be ground off in order to unthread the nut. Clamp the piston rod in shaft blocks and a vise, and unthread the retaining nut. Discard the old mid valve and spray the metal particles off of the piston rod with brake cleaner. The MX-Tech mid valve kit is prepackaged, so you can just remove the wire tie and slide the whole assembly right onto the stem, apply a small amount of Blue Loctite, and tighten down the nut.

The mid valve fits on the end of the cylinder rod and is retained by a nut. The MX-Tech valve is pre-built to simply replace the stock parts by bolting it into place.

Installing an MX-Tech Base Valve Kit

The base valve is located under the fork cap. Aftermarket kits such as the MX-Tech, Pro-Action, Race-Tech, and RG3 are designed to improve the passive compression damping of the forks. Typical rider benefits include an increase in the bike's responsiveness to bumps and resistance to G-loading.

The base valve fits on the end of the fork cap stem and is retained by a 10-mm nut. To install a base valve kit the 10-mm nut has to be removed, but there is a peening on the end of the stem that has to be ground off on a bench-grinding wheel before the nut can be removed. Discard the old base valve and spray clean the metal particles off of the stem with brake cleaner. The aftermarket base valve kits are prepackaged, so you can just remove the wire tie and slide the whole assembly right onto the stem, apply a small amount of Blue Loctite, and tighten down the nut.

The stock nut is peened over a washer during manufacturing. In order to remove the nut of any shaft that contains a piston and valve assembly, you have to grind off the peened washer on a bench-grinding wheel. Then the nut can be unthreaded and replaced.

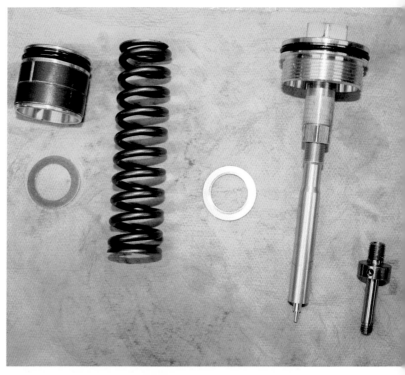

The base valve is clamped with the shaft blocks in a vise so the cap can be unthreaded and disassembled.

The base valve is threaded to the end of the main shaft. These are the other components of the base valve assembly: bushing and seal, internal compression spring (ICS), piston shaft, fork cap, and telescopic adjusting needle.

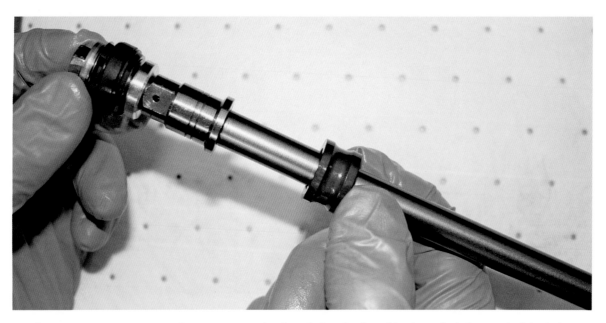

This is a travel limiter spacer. One or more can be threaded under the mid valve to limit the travel of the forks.

Chapter 13
WHEELS AND BRAKES

- How to Perform a Safety Check

- Installing a Pivot Works Wheel Bearing Kit

- Improving Braking with Oversized Disc Kits

- How to Install a Stainless Steel Brake Line

How to Perform a Safety Check

There are some key points to check on wheels and brakes. Spokes get loose, wheel bearings seize, brake fluid gets funky, brake pads wear down, discs get scored and bent, and flying rocks wreck everything!

Spokes: The spokes are tensioned fasteners. The spoke nipple seats into the rim and the spoke head seats into the hub. This seating will make the spokes loosen in tension, and if you don't keep the spokes tensioned equally, the rim will go out of true. New wheels take about two hours to break in, and spoke tension should be checked after the first few hours of use. The wheels come true from the factory, so as the spokes loosen, their trueness is best maintained by tightening each spoke a quarter-turn at a time, on every third spoke. After three rotations of the wheel, every spoke will be tensioned equally. All CRFs have 36 spokes. Once the wheels are broken in, check the spoke tension every three hours of riding. Take care not to over-tighten the spoke tension, because that can cause the rim to crack. Check the rim for cracks periodically.

Wheel bearings: Place your finger on the inside race and try to spin it. If the bearing is worn out, it will be hard to turn. Check for excessive movement in the race. A wheel bearing should never have any side-to-side movement! If it does, replace the wheel bearings and seals with a Pivot Works kit.

Brake fluid and pads: Brake fluid is hygroscopic and absorbs water over time, which can make the brake fluid boil and the caliper piston expand into the disc, causing the wheels to lock up. For best results use DOT 4 brake fluid and change it every 50 hours of riding time. Brake pads have wear indicators on them so you don't run them down to the metal backing, which could permanently damage the brake disc with deep scoring marks.

Discs: Brake discs get bent from hitting rocks. Moose Racing brake fins can do a good job at protecting the rear disc, but the front is the most vulnerable. You can tweak a bent disc back into shape with a large crescent wrench a limited number of times before it becomes break-hardened.

| PROJECT 29 | Installing a Pivot Works Wheel Bearing Kit |

Time: 15 minutes

Tools: Hammer, driver set, drift rod, grease, propane torch or heat gun, assembly oil

Talent: ★

Tab: $30

Parts: Pivot Works wheel bearing and seal kit

Benefits: Less rolling resistance, preventive maintenance against hub damage, better fuel consumption

1) Remove the seals from the wheel hub with a tire iron or screwdriver. Heat the hub around the spanner nut with a propane torch or heat gun.

2) Use a 1/4-inch drill on the four peen marks and drill to a depth of 1/8 inch to relieve the pressure on the spanner nut from the hub. This will enable you to unthread the spanner nut without stripping the threads.

3) Wheel bearings have an interference fit into the hubs. That means that the bearing is larger than the hole it fits into in the hub. The hub must be heated with a propane torch in the area around

These are the parts included in a Pivot Works wheel bearing rebuild kit for the CRF250X. The wheel has a long aluminum tube spacer to separate the left- and right-side bearings and seals. Pivot Works bearings are greased and sealed, so they're maintenance free.

Bearings have an interference fit to the hub; they are 0.002 inch larger than the hub. Heat the hub around the bearing so it expands a bit before you try to pound it out.

the bearing so that the hub will expand enough to allow the race to be removed. Unthread the spanner nut by tapping it counterclockwise with a drift-rod and hammer.

4) After the hub has been heated with a propane torch for about three minutes, use the following procedure to remove the bearings. From the back side, position a long drift rod onto the inner race of the bearing and strike it with a hammer; rotate the

position of the drift rod around the circumference of the race so you push the bearing out of the hub evenly.

5) The wheel-bearing assembly consists of two seals on each end, two to three wheel bearings, and one axle spacer. After removing one bearing, pull out the axle spacer. Then remove the second bearing. Notice how dirty and corroded the bearings and spacer become when the seals fail?

Honda stakes four marks around the outside of each wheel bearing as a safety measure to retain the bearing race. Drill the dimpled stake makes to remove the mark.

A spanner nut holds the bearing in the hub on just one side. The nut isn't very tight, but you can prep it by heating the area around it and spraying the threads with penetrating oil. Use a hammer and punch to spin it out counterclockwise.

6) Clean the inside of the hub, and then heat it with a propane torch for about three minutes, just prior to installing the bearing.
7) The Pivot Works bearings are greased and sealed, so don't attempt to remove the seals and grease them. Put them in the freezer for three hours to contract them to a smaller size.
8) Use a hammer and a bearing driver to install one bearing. Install the axle spacer, and then install the second bearing until it is fully seated. Install the seals and add a dab of grease, and you're done!

Use a long drift rod to force the center bushing off-center so the rod contacts the inner race of the opposite-side bearing. Once you get one bearing out, you'll have a clear shot at the second bearing.

The best way to install a wheel bearing is to freeze the bearing, heat the hub, coat the bearing with oil, and use a hydraulic press. The hammer method requires fewer tools but more finesse. You have to use a soft aluminum slug and hammer the bearing down evenly.

The spanner nut should be coated in grease or anti-seize and threaded in tightly.

PROJECT 30 | Improving Braking with Oversized Disc Kits

Time: 1 hour

Tools: Ratchet and sockets 10, 12, 22 mm, 10-mm 6-point box wrench

Talent: ★

Tab: $285

Parts: Braking or Moto-Master

Benefits: Improved braking performance

Improving Braking with Oversized Disc Kits

Moto-Master and Braking offer oversized front brake rotors and caliper brackets. If your stock disc is bent, or scored from running the pad down too far, then you might as well upgrade to a larger brake disc. Oversize brake kits include a new caliper bracket because with a larger-diameter disc you need to space the caliper back farther from the axle center for the proper clearance. The intermediary brackets require you to fasten the caliper to the bracket and the bracket to the fork leg.

Moto-Master makes heavier discs to absorb more thermal energy and are thus the choice of supermoto racers, whereas Braking discs are lightweight, wave-shaped, and made of stainless steel, so they are ideal for motocross. The fit and finish on Moto-Master discs are excellent. Braking kits may require a bit of patience and filing to get the bracket to fit properly. With either kit you can expect a marked improvement in front-braking performance.

1) Place the bike on a stand to elevate the front wheel and prepare to remove the front wheel and the caliper.
2) Loosen the two axle pinch bolts on the left fork leg with a 10-mm socket. Use a 22-mm socket to loosen the axle. Loosen and remove the two caliper bots with a 12-mm socket.
3) Use a 10-mm socket and 6-point box wrench to loosen and remove the disc mounting bolts.
4) Clean the new disc with brake cleaner to remove the protective coating.
5) Install the disc and torque the bolts to 100 in/lbs.
6) Apply a thin coating of grease on the axle and install the front wheel.

Tighten the axle to 55 ft-lbs of torque. Loosen the axle clamp pinch bolts on the right fork leg.

7) Install the new caliper bracket and torque the bolts to 18 ft-lbs.
8) Take the bike off the stand, hold the front brake, and pump the forks up and down. This will help to align the fork legs parallel on the front axle.
9) Tighten all four axle clamp pinch bolts to 18 ft-lbs.

Moto-Master makes a line of oversized discs, calipers, and brackets to fit CRF250 and 450s.

Braking discs are wave shaped and made of stainless steel.

Braking includes caliper brackets with their oversized brake kit.

How to Install a Stainless Steel Brake Line

Time: 20 minutes

Tools: Motion Pro bleeder kit, number 2 Phillips screwdriver, open-end wrenches 10 and 14 mm

Talent: ★

Tab: $75

Parts: Moose Racing stainless steel brake line, DOT 4 brake fluid, four new copper washers

Benefits: Better braking performance with a more durable brake line

A Moose Racing stainless steel brake line is puncture resistant and has less expansion when the brake is operated, which gives better braking performance. Here are some tips on installing this excellent product. This procedure works for front or rear brake lines.

1) Unthread the two 12-mm banjo bolts on the caliper and the master cylinder. Strip off the cable guide so you can remove the line.
2) Cap the bottom end of the new brake line with your fingers and use a small-diameter squirt bottle to fill the brake line from the top, priming it to reduce the air-bleeding time.
3) Install the stainless steel brake line with new copper washer gaskets and try not to spill too much fluid from the line.
4) Fill the master cylinder with DOT 4 brake fluid and install a Motion Pro bleeder kit to the caliper side of the brake line. Pump the brake lever, hold it firmly, and then crack loose the bleeder bolt to expunge any air in the line. Do this several times until the system is completely bled of air. Keep topping the master cylinder with brake fluid as you bleed the system.

Above: Bleed the brakes after you install your new stainless steel lines. Use clear plastic hose to route the fluid from the nipple on the caliper to your catch bottle. Squeeze the brake lever and loosen the bleeding nipple on the caliper for about one second.

Left: Keep adding fluid to the reservoir as you go. Once the fluid comes out of the caliper with no bubbles visible in the clear hose, you are getting close. Bleeding brakes requires that you keep doing this for quite some time—be patient.

Chapter 14
GRAPHIC CUSTOMIZATION

• Making Mock-ups and Ordering Graphics • Installing Graphic Sticker Kits

The latest style trend in dirt biking is custom graphics. Racers, teams, and businesses are all choosing graphics to highlight and promote themselves, sponsors, and businesses. Companies like Throttle Jockey, N-Style, and DeCal specialize in short-order team graphics, but DeCal has pioneered the one-off, custom-graphics concept.

The main reason for this custom-graphics trend is the influx of sponsorship into the sport and the need for differentiation. Here is an overview of how we designed custom graphics for our team bikes.

Make a Mock-up

If you're ordering custom graphics, there will be artwork and setup charges that are billed by the hour. To save yourself money and get the best possible job, you first need to make mock-ups of your basic graphic concept. Pass these sketches on to an artist who can produce your idea in an electronic format that can be printed to 3M sticker material.

Buy some sheets of large white or colored paper from an office supply store. Trace the shape of the radiator scoops, fenders, and side panels on the paper and cut out several sets of the shapes. Use double-sided tape to stick the paper to the bike, and use markers to draw the shapes and logos to get an idea of what they'll look like from a distance. Another trick is to photocopy logos and reduce or enlarge them, cut the shapes out, and tape them to the mock-up panels. DeCal has many popular logos in EPS and bitmap file formats that can easily be arranged to fit shapes like fenders, rad scoops, fork guards, swingarms, number plates, and seat covers. Once you determine what pattern you want, you can mail them to DeCal for their in-house artist to reproduce in an overall drawing of your bike so you can approve or amend the design. Expect to pay $150 to $300 for custom artwork.

Ordering Custom Graphics

Although DeCal offers 48-hour delivery on standard graphics, custom artwork takes at least two weeks because of the complexity of the task. Ordering several sets of graphics for your team helps you amortize the up-front costs of artwork and setup.

PROJECT 31

Installing Graphic Sticker Kits

Time: 30 minutes

Tools: Brake cleaner, window cleaner, and a scraper

Talent: ★

Tab: $50-200

Parts: Graphics kit

Benefits: Highlight your sponsors and team

Surface Prep

DeCal offers an installation kit for $14.95 that includes a plastic cleaner, surface prep, and a plastic scraper to press out all the air bubbles. Spray the surface of all the plastic parts with the cleaner, wipe dry, and spray on the installation fluid. The fluid will help enable you to adjust the stickers to the correct position and remove air bubbles.

Keep It Straight!

The best way to keep the stickers straight while applying them is to remove a small section of the backing

Vet rider Bill Zeisk customized his CRF250 with graphics that feature his business, Top Side Roofing, and his supporters. DeCal Works took it from concept drawing to finished product.

paper and align the still-covered part of the sticker on the plastic. Once you have it exactly where you want it, press down the exposed part of the sticker. Now, carefully peel off the backing while pressing down the sticker. This will help ensure that no air bubbles get trapped between the sticker and the plastic. If some air bubbles get trapped under the sticker, you can remove them by scraping them out to the edges with a plastic wedge tool.

Care for New Stickers

Stickers will eventually start to peel at the edges. Here are some tips on reducing the wear and tear on stickers. Don't pressure-wash the stickers directly at the edges. Also, be careful not to use harsh detergents meant for stripping grease from metal parts. These detergents will deteriorate the adhesives in the stickers. The best way to clean the stickers is with a sponge and water. If the edges of the sticker start peeling, use a razor knife to remove the peeled part of the sticker.

Eric Bleed of DeCal Works preps new plastic by spraying it with a light coating of brake cleaner, wiped dry with a clean paper towel, and a coating of window cleaner so the sticker has something to slide on.

DeCal Works had many logos on file, but other logos had to be scanned from stickers and letterhead, or designed from scratch.

DeCal Works includes a plastic scraper with each order. Wrap a bit of clean paper towel over the scraper and work out all of the air bubbles trapped between the sticker and plastic. Eventually, you will squeeze out all of the air and window cleaner to the edges of the sticker.

These semi-custom graphics are sold in a collectible kit form with the plastic, seat cover, and even a helmet. The kit is for CRF250 and 450s and is a replica of David Bailey's factory Honda circa 1986, available from One Industries.

Graphics specialist companies like Throttle Jockey, N-Style, and One Industries sell replica team graphics for their sponsored riders.

Resources

ACERBIS www.acerbis.com (800) 659-1440
Manufacturer of plastic body parts and lighting kits.

A-LOOP OFF-ROAD www.aloop.com (800) 662-5667
Distributor of GPS systems and mapping software for off-road motorcycling.

AMERICAN KOWA SEIKI www.kowatools.com (800) 824-9655
Manufacturer and distributor of special tools for engine and suspension servicing.

AMERICAN HONDA MOTOR CO. www.hondamotorcycle.com (310) 783-2000
Importer and distributor of Honda motorcycles.

ANSWER RACING www.answerracing.com (800) 840-3040
Manufacturer of Pro-Taper handlebars.

APPLIED RACING www.appliedrace.com (800) 853-0555
Manufacturer of aftermarket triple clamps.

ARC LEVERS www.arclevers.com (800) 204-7411
Manufacturer of fold-back levers.

BAJA DESIGNS www.bajadesigns.com (800) 422-5292
Distributor of wide ratio transmission kits, oil tanks, dual-sport kits, and guards.

BBR MOTORSPORTS www.bbrmotorsports.com (253) 631-8233
Manufacturer of trick billet parts for CRFs.

BIG BUN EXHAUST www.biggunexhaust.com (909) 948-7029
Manufacturer of exhaust systems.

BOYESEN ENGINEERING www.boyesen.com (800) 441-1177
Manufacturer of aluminum side covers and Quick-Shot accelerator pump covers.

BRAKING USA www.brakingusa.com (800) 272-5342
Manufacturer of brake rotors, oversized caliper brackets, and pads.

BRP www.brpit.com (800) 834-9363
Manufacturer of off-road gear for CRFs.

BUCHANAN WHEEL www.buchananspokes.com (626) 969-4655
Custom wheel builders.

CEET TECHNOLOGY www.ceetracing.com (760) 599-0111
Manufacturer of graphics kits, tall foam and seat covers.

CLARKE MANUFACTURING www.clarkemfg.com (503) 829-2156
Manufacturers of oversized off-road fuel tanks.

CV4 www.cv4.net (336) 472-2242
Manufacturer and distributor for Xceledyne valves, colored silicon hoses, and Fluidyne radiators.

DECAL WORKS www.socaldecal.com (800) 843-8244
Custom graphics specialists.

DEVOL ENGINEERING www.devolracing.com (800) 338-6599
Manufacturer of off-road guards and linkage kits.

DRUSSEL WILFREY DESIGN www.revloc.com (303) 292-1366
Manufacturer of REVLOC auto clutch kits.

ELECTREX www.electrexusa.com (888) 369-8359
Manufacturer of lighting coils and dual sport kits.

ENZO RACING (714) 541-5218
Suspension specialist, distributor of air tanks.

FACTORY CONNECTION www.factoryconnection.com (800) 221-7560
Suspension specialists and manufacturer of trick billet suspension parts.

FASTWAY PERFORMANCE www.fastwayperformance.com (503) 244-8368
Manufacturer of ergonomic foot pegs and clutch cable brackets.

FORWARD MOTION www.forwardmotion.com.mx (630) 825-5645
Author Eric Gorr's company, specializing in CRF performance.

HINSON RACING www.hinsonracing.com (909) 946-2942
Manufacturer of high performance clutch parts.

IMS PRODUCTS www.imsproducts.com (909) 653-7720
Distributor of off-road products for CRFs.

KEHIN FUEL SYSTEMS www.kehin-usa.com (262) 860-6000
Importers for Kehin carburetors.

KIBBLEWHITE PRECISION MACHINING www.blackdiamondvalves.com (650) 359-4704 Manufacturer of valve train parts.

L.A. SLEEVE www.lasleeveco.com (562) 945-7578
Manufacturers and distributors of performance engine parts.

MAGURA www.magurausa.com (800) 448-3876
Manufacturers of hydraulic clutch kits and oversized handlebars.

METTEC www.mettec.com (775) 246-8200
Manufacturer of lightweight titanium axles and fasteners for CRFs.

MOOSE RACING www.mooseracing.com
The off-road division of Parts Unlimited.

MOTION PRO www.motionpro.com (650) 594-9600
Manufacturers of specialty tools and control cables.

MOTO-MASTER www.motomasterusa.com (866) MOTOMAS
Manufacturers of brake calipers, brackets, and disc rotors.

MT RACING www.mtracing.com (909) 353-1253
Importers for Vortex ignition systems.

MX-TECH www.mx-tech.com (815) 936-6277
Manufacturers of aftermarket suspension products and valving kits.

OHLINS www.ohlins.com
Manufacturers of suspension components and steering dampers.

ONE INDUSTRIES www.oneindustries.com (858) 874-5760
Manufacturers of graphics and seat covers.

PIVOT WORKS www.pivotworks.com (888) 632-5617
Manufacturers of rebuild kits for forks, steering and linkage bearings.

PRO CIRCUIT www.procircuit.com (909) 738-8050
Manufacturer and distributor of exhaust systems and trick billet parts.

PRO MOTO BILLET www.promotobillet.com (208) 377-8747
Manufacturer of trick billet parts including kick-stands, guards, and silencer tips.

PRO-ACTION www.pro-action.com (888) 698-8990
Suspension specialists, franchises worldwide.

RACE TECH www.race-tech.com (951) 279-6655
Manufacturer and distributor of suspension tools and performance parts.

SCOTT'S PERFORMANCE www.scottsperformance.com (818) 248-6747 Distributors of steering dampers and stainless steel oil filters.

SDG Seats www.sdgusa.com (714) 258-1224
Manufacturer of ergonomic seats.

SERVICE HONDA www.servicehonda.com (219) 932-3588
Custom CRF builders and discount mail-order Honda parts.

SFB RACING www.sfbracing.ca
Manufacturer of trick billet side covers, Powerblades, and flywheel weights.

SRS www.srsracing.it (631) 725-5726
Manufacturer of trick parts for CRFs, made in Italy.

STEAHLY OFF-ROAD PRODUCTS www.steahlyoffroad.com (800) 800-2363
Manufacturers of off-road guards, racks, and flywheel weights.

THROTTLE JOCKEY www.throttlejockey.com (800) 847-6885
Manufacturers of custom graphics and seat covers.

THUMPER RACING www.thumperracingusa.com (800) 259-5186
CRF performance specialists.

US CHROME www.usnicom.com (920) 922-5066
Cylinder replating and big bore kits.

VARNER MOTORSPORTS www.varnermotorsports.com (909) 608-2103
CRF performance specialists.

WISECO www.wisecopiston.com (800) 321-1364
Manufacturer of performance pistons, crankshafts, and clutch parts.

WORKS ENDURO RIDER (W.E.R.) www.werproducts.com (908) 637-6385
Manufacturer of steering dampers and other durable hard parts for off-road.

Index

The Best Tools for the Job.

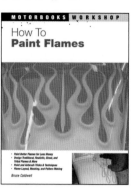

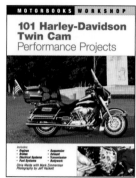
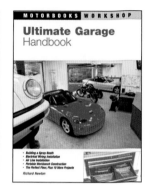

Other Great Books in this Series